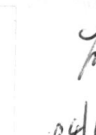
AS/A2
Music Technology
Listening Tests

Second Edition

239–241 Shaftesbury Avenue
London WC2H 8TF
Telephone: 020 7333 1720
Fax: 020 7333 1765

www.rhinegold.co.uk

Music Study Guides

GCSE, AS and A2 Music Study Guides (AQA, Edexcel and OCR)
GCSE, AS and A2 Music Listening Tests (AQA, Edexcel and OCR)
GCSE Music Study Guide (WJEC)
GCSE Music Listening Tests (WJEC)
AS/A2 Music Technology Study Guide (Edexcel)
AS/A2 Music Technology Listening Tests (Edexcel)
Revision Guides for GCSE (AQA, Edexcel and OCR), AS and A2 Music (Edexcel)

Also available from Rhinegold Education

Key Stage 3 Listening Tests: Book 1 and Book 2
AS and A2 Music Harmony Workbooks
GCSE and AS Music Composition Workbooks
GCSE and AS Music Literacy Workbooks
Romanticism in Focus, Baroque Music in Focus, Film Music in Focus,
Modernism in Focus, *The Immaculate Collection* in Focus, *Who's Next* in Focus,
Batman in Focus, *Goldfinger* in Focus, Musicals in Focus,
Music Technology from Scratch

Rhinegold also publishes Choir & Organ, Classical Music, Classroom Music, Early Music Today, International Piano, Music Teacher, Muso, Opera Now, Piano, Teaching Drama, British and International Music Yearbook, British Performing Arts Yearbook, British Music Education Yearbook, World Conservatoires, Rhinegold Dictionary of Music in Sound

Other Rhinegold Study Guides

Rhinegold publishes resources for candidates studying Drama and Theatre Studies.

First published 2010 in Great Britain by
Rhinegold Publishing Ltd
239-241 Shaftesbury Avenue
London WC2H 8TF
Telephone: 020 7333 1720
Fax: 020 7333 1765
www.rhinegold.co.uk

Rhinegold Publishing Ltd has used its best efforts in preparing this workbook. It does not assume,
and hereby disclaims, any liability to any party for loss or damage caused by errors or omissions in the guide
whether such errors or omissions result from negligence, accident or other cause.

You should always check the current requirements of the examination, since these may change. Copies of the
Edexcel specification can be downloaded from the Edexcel website at www.edexcel.com.
Edexcel Publications telephone: 01623 467467, fax: 01623 450481, email: publications@linney.com.

Edexcel AS/A2 Music Technology Listening Tests

British Library Cataloguing in Publication Data.
A catalogue record for this book is available from the British Library.
ISBN: 978-1-906178-90-1
Printed in Great Britain by Halstan

Contents

The authors

Alan Charlton is a freelance composer. He was awarded the first ever PhD in Composition from Bristol University in 1997 and was the first Eileen Norris Fellow in Composition at Bedford School (1999–2002). He was head of music technology at Bedford School from 2000–2009 and is also an examiner for Edexcel.

Alec Boulton is a freelance music teacher, studio-design consultant, recording producer, pianist and composer. He delivers music technology (KS workshops through to A level) in a number of schools in London. He is also company director of Route 430 Ltd.

Acknowledgements

The authors would like to thank Edexcel Principal Examiner Lloyd Russell for his invaluable help as consultant, and the Rhinegold editorial team of Matthew Hammond, Katherine Smith and Chris Elcombe for their expert support in the preparation of this book.

For the audio CD, Alec Boulton would also like to thank the following artists: Karlene ('Sorry' vocals); BillyBottle ('Holler' vocals, piano, bass, drums, and 'Mercutio' guitar); Martine Waltier ('Mercutio' vocals); Steve Watts ('Mercutio' bass), Martin Hoj (consultant and test candidate).

Audio Tracks

An accompanying CD is available (RHG319) which contains all the tracks relating to the **A2** listening tests. Please note that all our books are now distributed by Music Sales. If you wish to buy online, you will be directed from our website through to www.musicroom.com. Alternatively, please call 01284 725 725 (01284 773 666 for schools).

All extracts used for the **AS** listening tests are available to buy online via **iTunes**. Please note there is no audio CD to accompany the AS portion of the book.

To purchase or download the album online please go to the Edexcel AS/A2 Music Technology Listening Tests page at www.listeningtests.co.uk where you will find a direct link to the iTunes store.

To download iTunes and set up an account go to www.apple.com/itunes/download/. For help and advice on using iTunes or setting up an account, go to the Edexcel AS/A2 Music Technology Listening Tests page at www.listeningtests.co.uk.

Copyright

AS level

Introduction

The listening tests for AS-level Music Technology are worth 30% of the total AS marks. They are designed to test your knowledge of AoS 1: The Principles and Practice of Music Technology and AoS 2: Popular Music Styles since 1910. The AS listening paper is split into two sections, each of which is worth 40 marks. Section A consists of four questions on the musical and technological features of extracts of popular music from 1910 to the present day. Section B questions look at two set styles in more detail, for which you will need more in-depth knowledge.

For both section A and section B questions, you will require:

➤ Aural skills
➤ Knowledge of musical features and terminology
➤ Understanding of sequencing, recording and production techniques
➤ The ability to recognise instrumentation and instrumental techniques used in popular music
➤ A broad overview of the key developments in the history of music technology.

The AS part of this book looks at section A and section B questions separately. By working through a number of these questions, you will soon become familiar with what you might be expected to answer in the exam. This will help you to identify which areas you may need to focus on to improve your exam performance and will familiarise you with the types of question you may be asked. Hints are provided for many of the questions. Don't worry if the questions seem a little daunting at first: with practice, answering them will become second nature. They are also an excellent excuse to get to know a wide range of songs in detail: the knowledge you gain by seeing how the music has been put together can help you to create and perform your own music and to appreciate other music better.

Section A questions

Overview

Section A questions concentrate on the practical and musical skills you acquire while completing the coursework tasks. For most of these questions, you will need to demonstrate that you can use appropriate **terminology**: the technical terms for features of music and production that are used in the music industry. It is very helpful for you to get into the habit of using correct terminology as it will not only help your exam performance, it will make you sound more authoritative when talking about your own or other people's music!

When you come across a term you do not understand, find out what it means and try to use it yourself at the next opportunity. It is well worth keeping a notebook in which to write down these words.

Question types

Aural notation questions

These test you on your ability to write down accurately specific musical features of a song, using musical or sequencer-based notation. You may be asked to do the following:

➤ Identify the tempo
➤ Identify the time signature
➤ Fill in the missing pitches
➤ Complete the rhythm
➤ Identify the interval between two parts

➢ Complete the chord progression
➢ Specify whether the music is major or minor.

If you are also studying AS Music or are taking instrumental grade exams, you should be familiar with most of these types of question. However, even if you are not very confident about your music reading skills, you can still pick up marks by thinking logically. Use the hints provided in the questions, and ask your teacher for more help and further practice to give you more confidence. If you have access to it, ear-training software can also help you.

Musical description questions

➢ Identify the instrument
➢ Identify the playing/singing technique
➢ Describe the texture
➢ Describe the structure
➢ Describe the musical device.

For these questions you do not need to be able to read staff notation, but you do need to know what a wide range of instruments sound like. You should be able to identify standard techniques on guitar, drums, voice, stringed instruments, wind instruments and turntables.

For longer questions, there is a knack of writing descriptions in a clear, concise way. Once you have answered a question, look at the answer at the back of the book. Have you made all the points in the suggested answer and is there a better way of putting them, either by rephrasing them or using different terminology? Then, if necessary, write out your answer to the question again, aiming to make it clearer.

Recording techniques questions

➢ Describe or comment on a particular recording technique
➢ Explain how a recording could be improved or made differently using modern equipment.

For these questions, you need to be able to draw on your experience of microphone types and positions that you have used in your recording coursework. There may be some you have not encountered: make sure you know the standard set-ups for the common popular music instruments such as acoustic and electric guitar, bass guitar, drum kit, vocals, upright and grand piano, brass and wind instruments and small groups of performers such as a horn section or backing vocalists.

You also need to be familiar with recording techniques from the past and their limitations. Be aware, too, of different microphone types and pick-up patterns, and devices such as DI boxes, pop shields, amplifiers and amp simulators. You might occasionally be asked about logistical problems you might encounter, such as minimising spill: draw on your practical experience and common sense to answer this.

Production questions

➢ Identify the effect, process or mixing technique
➢ Describe how a production technique might be used to make or improve a recording.

You should have encountered most of the common production features in your sequencing and recording coursework. As well as being able to identify the sounds of reverb, delay, flanging, chorus, vocoder, autotune, compression, gating and so on, you will also need to know how they work and which parameters can be adjusted. Panning questions ask you to place instruments in the stereo field and identify techniques such as autopan and double tracking. You may also be asked questions on EQ and the balance between different tracks.

Sequencing, synthesis and sampling-related questions

➢ Describe how the music would be inputted and edited in a sequencer

➢ Explain the terminology
➢ Identify the MIDI process
➢ Identify the sampling/synthesis concept.

These cover concepts you might encounter in your sequencing work: the standard editors (track editor, key editor, drum editor and score editor), the basic controllers (volume, pan, modulation, sustain), pitch-bends, common insert effects (reverb, double delay, etc.) and ways in which you might manipulate MIDI data. You should also understand how synthesisers work, together with relevant terminology (ADSR, LFO, SMPTE, VCO, VCF). Finally, you should have a basic grasp of sampling terminology: retriggering, loops, multi-timbral instruments and velocity-sensitive samplers. Make sure you can explain what the differences are between a sequencer, a synthesiser and a sampler!

Questions on musical styles

➢ Identify the style
➢ Choose a band of the same/different style
➢ List features of the style.

As style is covered in more detail in section B, any style questions in section A will probably be fairly brief, perhaps limited to one or two marks. It is nevertheless essential to learn the characteristics of different styles, the names of the major figures and bands associated with the style, the date, location and social setting in which they were popular and their influence on other styles. This knowledge will enable you to expect what to look out for when hearing certain types of music and also enable you to spot stylistic influences, such as a gospel influence in a soul song. It will also help you to place the set styles for section B in context.

The questions in section A of this book cover a range of styles, but you should also back this up by reading a historical overview in a textbook such as Rhinegold's *AS/A2 Music Technology Study Guide* (second edition, ISBN: 978-1-906178-48-2), listening to relevant tracks to reinforce your knowledge.

History-related questions

➢ Choose the date of the recording.

You may be asked to circle the correct date of a recording. You can make an educated guess at this if you know how music technology developed over the years and when different styles were dominant. For instance, if the recording is in stereo, you can assume it was made after 1960; if it uses a primitive-sounding electronic drum machine, it probably dates from the early 1980s. Make sure you know the dates when important developments took place: the electric guitar, stereo recording, multi-track recording, digital recording, the drum machine, sampler and computer sequencer. It is useful to know when certain styles were popular: rock 'n' roll in the mid to late 1950s, disco in the mid to late 1970s and so on.

Recording quality is also a clue, especially with older tracks: listen out for a reduced frequency response, crackle and distortion. Finally, certain instrumental sounds and styles of production were popular at different times: very wide panning, for instance, was often used in the late 1960s and early 1970s, snare with gated reverb in the 1980s and autotuned voice after 2000. If you find out the date of every song you hear, you will soon find that certain eras have a particular 'sound' which you should eventually be able to identify more or less instinctively.

Hints on question styles

Multiple choice: if you do not know the answer, try to eliminate choices that you definitely know to be wrong.

Complete the rhythm/pitches: use a pencil and make your answer as neat as you can: avoid writing notes whose position on the stave is unclear.

Complete the table: short phrases are sufficient here. However, as in all answers, try to use terminology in your response, for example 'reduced high frequencies' is better than 'sounds muddy' and 'upward glissando' is better than 'slidey noise'. If they are not already given in the question, **always refer to specific instrument(s) and timings on the recording:** 'a delay effect is used' is too vague: 'a delay effect is used on the electric guitar at 0'34"' is much better.

Comparison questions: these will probably be in table form. Make sure you compare like with like: 'recording A includes a voice whereas recording B is fast' is not a valid comparison, whereas 'recording A includes a voice, whereas recording B substitutes a saxophone for this part' would be acceptable.

One-line answer: again, a short phrase will suffice.

Short answer: usually these carry two or more marks, and will require some sort of description or explanation. The rubric will tell you whether to use short sentences or bullet points.

In written answers, **always use appropriate terminology and include references to specific timings**.

Exam technique

If possible, try to answer questions in the same conditions you would experience in the exam. You must be listening on good-quality headphones and always check that they are the right way round before you begin. Your playback device must have a track-timing display in seconds. If possible, use the CD player you will use in the exam, although because the tracks in this book need to be downloaded from the internet, you may have to listen via a computer, MP3 player or iPod. Remember that pausing, rewinding and fast-forwarding can save you time and allow you to hone in on short sections, so do use these functions. Adjust the volume so that you can hear the music clearly. However, never listen at too loud a volume as you can seriously damage your hearing.

An important consideration is to look at the number of marks each question carries: this will be the number of relevant points you should aim to make to achieve full marks in that question.

How you use the available time is important in achieving a good mark. You have one hour and 45 minutes to answer the whole exam, so roughly 50 minutes for section A. Therefore, expect to spend about 10–12 minutes on each section A question. Look at the number of marks awarded for each individual question: try not to spend too long on questions that only carry one mark.

> More hints on exam technique can be found on page 96 of Rhinegold's *AS/A2 Music Technology Study Guide* (second edition).

Section B questions

Section B questions are based on the two specific styles that have been prescribed in the specification for your year of study. There are two section B questions, one on each style, and each is worth 20 marks. Together they are worth half of the total marks for the paper.

Approximately half of each section B question contains questions similar to section A questions, being based on the aural recognition of features of the music and production. However, they will tend to focus on features that are specific to each style. So, for instance, in rock 'n' roll, questions might concentrate on the shortcomings of early recordings and specific techniques that were used in the recording of rock 'n' roll, such as slap-back echo.

The remainder of each section B question is centred around the history and context of the specified style. Questions you might be asked include:

➢ The general features (musical and otherwise) of the style
➢ How the style originated
➢ How the style developed

➤ The influences the style had on other music
➤ The contribution of one or more artists to the style
➤ Innovations in the use of music technology that are associated with the style.

So how should you prepare for the section B questions? First, you need to read and absorb a thorough account of the style from an authoritative textbook. This will enable you to answer most of the questions above and give you a strong overview of the style. From this, you will have an idea of the key artists, bands, producers and record labels associated with that style. Select six to eight bands or artists to study in more detail. For each artist, you should be able to describe:

➤ The key features of their music (any musical trademarks of their style, their singing style, their performing style, the themes they explored with their lyrics)
➤ The names of important songs and albums in their output
➤ The dates when they were active
➤ The influence they had on other artists.

You should study one song by each artist in detail, so that you can refer to it to support any points you need to make about lyrics, musical style and so on.

Finally, the most important part of preparing for section B questions is to get to know in detail as many songs as you can in that style. This makes remembering facts, song titles and so on much simpler; it will make what you read about the style much easier to grasp; and it will enable you to think independently instead of regurgitating facts from a textbook.

Useful textbooks include Rhinegold's *AS/A2 Music Technology Study Guide* (second edition), which gives an overview of the main styles, and *Pop Music: the Textbook* (Edition Peters, EP7690).

AS level: section A questions

Question 1

Mudhoney: 'Let it Slide' from *Every Good Boy Deserves Fudge* (1991)   **(2'35")**

(a)   This track could be described as an example of **grunge**. Which of the following was **not** a grunge band?

Nirvana ☒   Soundgarden ☒   Black Sabbath ☒   Pearl Jam ☒   **(1)**

(b)   Describe the quality of electric guitar tone heard on the track.

....

.... **(2)**

> Think about how the guitarist might have set up their amplifier, and whether they have used any additional ways of altering the sound.

(c)   Name the effect heard on the clean electric guitar at 0'07".

Harmonic ☒   Feedback ☒   Skanking ☒   Dive bomb ☒   **(1)**

(d)   Describe how the lead vocal and lead guitar interact in the passage 0'14"–0'25".

....

.... **(2)**

(e)   What is the interval between the two voices from the lines 'Nobody's here to stay' to the word 'grave' at 0'54"–1'03"?

5ths ☒   3rds ☒   6ths ☒   Octaves ☒   **(1)**

(f)   The drums in this track have been recorded to produce a 'live' sound appropriate to the raw, energetic style of the music. Describe how microphone placement and choice of recording space could enable you to recreate this sound.

....

.... **(2)**

(g)   The two electric guitars have been panned far apart in this track. Why might this be important in this style of music?

.... **(1)**

(Total 10 marks)

Question 2

The Beach Boys: 'I Get Around' from *The Very Best of the Beach Boys* **(2001)** (2'14")

(a) Name the vocal technique used by the highest voice on the track.

.... (1)

(b) Mark with a cross the correct version of the rhythm played by the electric bass between 0'20" and 0'27". (1)

(i)  ☒

(ii)  ☒

(iii)  ☒

(iv) 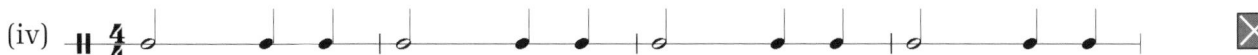 ☒

(c) From 0'20"–0'41" a change in the instrumentation is introduced every two bars. In the table below, describe a change in instrumentation for each two-bar section. The first two sections are completed for you. The timings are approximate. (4)

> Note that the question asks for changes in the instrumentation. Write down the most obvious change that you can hear in each section.

Timing	Change in instrumentation
0'20"	**Example:** lead vocal accompanied by bass
0'24"	**Example:** as above, but with clapping on each beat introduced
0'27"	
0'30"	
0'33"	
0'37"	

(d)   Which term most closely describes the style of singing that appears on the track from 0'55"–1'06"?

Doo-wop ☒   Scat ☒   Bebop ☒   A capella ☒   (1)

(e)   (i)   Describe how you would arrange a group of backing singers around a single omnidirectional microphone to obtain an effective balance.

....

....   (1)

(ii)   Name **two** limitations in recording a group of singers using a single microphone.

....

....   (2)

(Total 10 marks)

Recording exercise: try out the recording technique described in question (e) on a group of three to four singers, aiming for the most focused and well-balanced sound as possible. Experiment with the positioning of the singers, the placement of the microphone and different microphone types.

Note: this technique is provided for general interest only; it should not normally be used in coursework, because coursework should use contemporary recording techniques.

Question 3

Isaac Hayes: 'Theme from Shaft' from *Shaft* (1971)   **(4'36")**

(a) What is the name of the device that produces the characteristic effect in the rhythm guitar from 0'05" onwards?

....   **(1)**

(b) In the diagram below, draw in the correct position of the pan pots for the following instruments **in the section from 0'00"–1'16":** rhythm guitar; trumpet; hi-hat/ride cymbal; flute.   **(4)**

Rhythm guitar	Trumpet	Organ	Hi-hat/ride cymbal

Bass/keyboard	Flute	Trombone	Guitar (chords)

(c) Which is the correct version of the repeated hi-hat pattern that begins at 2'42"?   **(1)**

(i)   ☒

(ii)   ☒

(iii)   ☒

(iv)   ☒

(d) Comment on the panning of the lead guitar from 4'09"–4'28".

....

.... **(1)**

(e) The style of this track could be described as being a mixture of soul and funk. Name two musical characteristics of funk that can be heard on this track.

.... and .... **(2)**

(f) The tempo of this track fluctuates, becoming slightly faster towards the end. If you were to produce an exact copy of the track using a computer sequencer, how would you replicate these changes in tempo?

....

.... **(1)**

                                                 (Total 10 marks)

Question 4

Tammy Wynette: 'The Ways to Love a Man' from *Stand by Your Man: The Very Best of Tammy Wynette* (2008) (2'26")

(a) Select the correct time signature of the song.

$\frac{3}{4}$ ☒ $\frac{9}{8}$ ☒ $\frac{12}{8}$ ☒ $\frac{2}{4}$ ☒   **(1)**

(b) What is the name of the solo instrument heard in the introduction (0'00"–0'10")?

.... **(1)**

(c) Insert the following chords into the correct boxes in the table below to match those of the accompaniment from 0'11"–0'52". **(4)**

A♭ major; C major; D♭ major; E♭ major

Timing of beginning of phrase	1st bar of phrase	2nd bar of phrase	3rd bar of phrase	4th bar of phrase
Phrase 1 (0'11"–0'20")	A♭	D♭	A♭	A♭7
Phrase 2 (0'21"–0'32")		E♭		A♭7
Phrase 3 (0'32"–0'41")	D♭			D♭
Phrase 4 (0'42"–0'52")	A♭	D♭	A♭	D♭

(d) The keyboard heard at the beginning of the track features a tremolo effect. How could you achieve a similar effect on a soft synth through the use of a low frequency oscillator (LFO)?

Setting the LFO to control the:

Pitch ☒   Velocity ☒   Panning ☒   Volume ☒   **(1)**

(e) Which of the following words most closely describes the style of this track?

Blues ☒   Folk ☒   Soul ☒   Country ☒   **(1)**

(f) Describe **two** changes in the arrangement that make the setting of the phrase 'it is hard to change your mind' (0'36") stand out from the music that immediately precedes it.

....

.... **(2)**

(Total 10 marks)

Sequencing exercise: sequence the opening of the song. Practise inputting pitch-bends by sequencing the instrument identified in question (b), choosing an appropriate software instrument. Copy the pitch-bends and tone of the instrument as accurately as possible. (You may need to change the pitch-bend range of your chosen software instrument; the controller setting for this can usually be found in the software instrument's interface.) Try also to replicate the tremolo effect on the keyboard by using the method you identified in question (d).

Question 5

Queen: 'Killer Queen' from *Queen: The Singles Collection (Remastered)* (1981)   **(3'03")**

(a)   Name the effect used on the solo voice on the words 'laser beam' at 0'32"–0'34".

....   **(1)**

(b)   The production on this track makes creative use of the stereo field. In the table below, describe how the stereo field has been used creatively during the times indicated (an example is given for the first excerpt).   **(5)**

Start time	End time	How the stereo field is used
1'22"	1'26"	**Example:** Backing vocals on the phrases 'bah bah bah bah' and 'anytime' are panned respectively hard left and hard right
1'49"	2'02"	**(3)**
2'11"	2'17"	**(2)**

(c)   This track contains a recording of an upright piano. Describe a standard recording set-up for capturing the sound of an upright piano.

....

.... **(2)**

See page 51 of Rhinegold's *AS/A2 Music Technology Study Guide* for more information on recording pianos.

(d)   Identify the time signature in the section from 0'52"–1'07".

  $\frac{3}{4}$ ☒ $\frac{6}{8}$ ☒ $\frac{4}{4}$ ☒ $\frac{5}{4}$ ☒   **(1)**

(e)   Name the playing technique on the snare drum at 0'54"–0'56".

....   **(1)**

                                                                                                                    (Total 10 marks)

Question 6

Eurythmics: 'Who's That Girl' from *Eurythmics: Ultimate Collection* (2005)   (3'45")

(a) Fill in the missing pitches from the first seven notes of the melody heard in the upper register between 0'04" and 0'12", for which the rhythm is given. (Note that the pitches below are written an octave lower than they sound.)   **(3)**

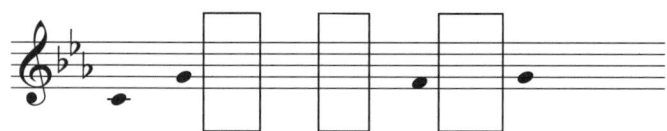

(b) How does the processing of the snare drum in the passage from 0'20"–0'51" differ from that in 0'52"–1'36"?

....

.... **(1)**

(c) The arrangement is given added textural interest through the overdubbing of different vocal parts against the main vocal line. In the table below, identify **three** instances of vocal overdubbing that occur between 0'37" and 1'09", explaining how the arranger has used the voices, and identifying production and mixing techniques used on these extra vocal parts.   **(6)**

Timing	Description of vocal arrangement	Production/mixing techniques used
0'37"–0'39"	**Example:** a second vocal part is added, which shadows the contour of the melody, and adding harmonies	**Example:** the capture is similar to that of the lead vocal, but it is set back in the mix slightly; it is panned slightly to the left.
0'52"–1'02"		
0'53"–0'55"		
0'58"–1'09"		

(Total 10 marks)

Question 7

Jimi Hendrix: 'Purple Haze' from *Experience Hendrix: the Best of Jimi Hendrix* (1997)   **(2'52")**

(a) The lowest guitar in the texture from 0'00"–0'23" plays a repeated note alternating between different octaves. What is the correct musical term for a held or repeated note whose pitch stays the same while harmonies above it are changing?

Riff ☒   Ostinato ☒   Pedal note ☒   Appoggiatura ☒   **(1)**

(b) Name the downwards sliding effect that occurs four times between 0'09" and 0'24".

....   **(1)**

(c) This track is an example of **psychedelic rock**. Describe **two** features of the production and **two** features of the musical arrangement which might suggest a disorientated, drug-induced state.   **(4)**

Timing	Instrument	Production feature
0'33"–1'10"	Lead vocals	**Example:** lead vocals panned to right, and have added delay and reverb
1'37"–1'53"	Spoken 'ooh' and 'ah' sounds	
2'36"–2'50"	Guitar tremolo note	

(Describe **two** features)

Timing	Feature	Musical feature
0'00"–0'06"	Harmony	**Example:** Use of tritones/augmented 4ths/dissonant intervals in opening staccato chords
1'13"–1'36"	Melody	
2'23"–2'50"	Texture	

(Describe **two** features)

(d) The style of Jimi Hendrix's singing in this track is particularly influenced by which of the following American singers?

Johnny Cash ☒   Jerry Lee Lewis ☒   Bob Dylan ☒   Frank Sinatra ☒   **(1)**

(e) Hendrix made extensive use of four-, eight- and 16-track tape recorders in producing his music, using techniques that would now be carried out on a computer sequencer. Identify **three** advantages of producing audio recordings on a computer sequencer over a multi-track tape recorder.

....

....

....   **(3)**

(Total 10 marks)

Question 8

Jelly Roll Morton and His Orchestra: 'Try Me Out' from *Jelly Roll Morton – Vol.II* (2006) (2'32")

(a) Which word most closely describes the style of this music?

Swing ☒   New Orleans jazz ☒   Blues ☒   Bebop ☒   (1)

(b) The accompaniment of this track in the section from 0'59"–1'18" is based on a piano playing style called **stride**. Briefly describe the most important feature of stride.

....

.... (1)

(c) In the diagram of a mixing desk below, mark in the approximate fader positions for the instruments shown in the passage from 1'42"–2'04". (3)

Tuba   Piano   Banjo   Clarinet

(d) This is a remastered version of a recording from 1929, released in 2006. Name **two** shortcomings of a vintage recording like this and explain how the recording could be cleaned up using present-day technology. (4)

Shortcoming	How it could be improved
Example: 'wow' producing variations in pitch	Use time-stretching to cancel out the variations in speed

(e) On which speed of vinyl record would this recording have originally been released?

16⅔ rpm   33 rpm   45 rpm   78 rpm   (1)

(Total 10 marks)

Recording exercise: in early recordings, there was no way of altering the balance between instruments apart from arranging them different distances away from the horn of the recording device. Using a single microphone, capture a mono recording of two or three instruments or voices of contrasting volumes (for instance a drum kit, a singer and a trumpet), aiming to achieve the best balance as possible solely by placing the performers at different distances from the microphone.

Question 9

Rev. James Cleveland: 'Get Right Church' from *Gospel Music* (2006)   **(3'20")**

(a) Two keyboard instruments can be heard on this track, one of which is a piano. What is the name of the second instrument?

   Ondes martenot ☒   Minimoog ☒   Clavinet ☒   Hammond organ ☒   **(1)**

(b) What is the tempo of this song?

   69bpm ☒   84bpm ☒   112bpm ☒   132bpm ☒   **(1)**

(c) Which of the following rhythms most closely represents the rhythm of the lead vocalist's repeated phrase 'alleluia' in the section from 2'13"–2'21"?

   (i)   ☒

   (ii)   ☒

   (iii) ☒

   (iv)   ☒   **(1)**

(d) Describe the interaction between the vocal soloist and the choir from 0'08"– 0'21".

   ....

   .... **(2)**

> The fact that there are two marks for this question tells you that it is not a straightforward answer, and will require you to make two points.

(e) What features of the music that can be heard on this track identify it with the gospel style?

   ....

   ....

   .... **(3)**

(f) Identify **one** shortcoming of the capture of the choir on the recording and briefly describe how this problem could be solved if the track were to be re-recorded.

   ....

   .... **(2)**

(Total 10 marks)

> **Recording exercise:** using just a solo singer, attempt to simulate the effect of a whole chorus, singing a short phrase such as 'Get Right Church', by using overdubbing. You will need at least ten different versions of the track. You may find it quickest to set the sequencer to record on a loop and perform all the different versions in one take. Pan the different takes across the stereo field and add reverb to give the impression of a chorus standing at a distance. You can also try the same technique to record hand-claps.

Question 10

Rihanna: 'Umbrella (Radio Edit)' from *Umbrella* (2007)   **(4'15")**

(a) Which genre most closely describes the style of this song?

    R&B ☒   Hip hop ☒   Soul ☒   Big beat ☒   **(1)**

(b) Which term best describes the male artist's vocal technique that occurs on this track from 0'00" to 0'34"?

    ....   **(1)**

(c) Complete the missing pitches of the bass line from 0'55"–1'07".   **(2)**

(d) Describe **two** effects applied to the lead vocal from 0'56"–1'17".

    ....

    .... **(2)**

(e) Describe **four** changes in instrumentation introduced into the musical arrangement in the section from 2'45"–3'02" that contrast with the preceding music.

    ....

    ....

    ....

    .... **(4)**

(Total 10 marks)

Composing/sequencing/recording exercise: compose a short section of a song inspired by the setting of the word 'umbrella' at 1'17"–1'40". Create a drum loop and input a four-bar chord sequence such as F–C–G–Am using a synth pad sound. Choose a word like 'umbrella' or a short phrase, then record someone singing your chosen word in time to your drum track. Using the Rihanna track as a guide, construct a rhythm from it, cutting up the sample into short fragments and copying and reassembling these in different orders, using quantisation to synchronise them with the drum track. Try also experimenting with pitch-shifting to create melodies.

Question 11

Slipknot: 'Wait and Bleed' from *Slipknot* (1999)   (2'28")

(a)   Which term best describes the style of the music?

   Punk rock ☒   Nu metal ☒   Indie rock ☒   Hip hop ☒   **(1)**

(b)   Which of the following is the correct version of the first four notes of the guitar part from 0'00" to 0'03"? (Note that these are written an octave higher than they sound.)   **(1)**

(i)   ☒

(ii)   ☒

(iii)   ☒

(iv)   ☒

(c)   Describe how the vocal line is made to sound progressively more threatening from the start of the song to 0'45". Refer to the musical arrangement and performance in your answer.

....

....

.... **(3)**

(d)   What is the interval between the two guitar parts from 2'17" to 2'26"?

   Octaves ☒   5ths ☒   3rds ☒   6ths ☒   **(1)**

(e)   This style of music makes extensive use of compression. In the table below, name **two** of the parameters that might be used when using a compressor and describe what each one does to the compressed signal.   **(4)**

Name of parameter	How it changes the signal
Make-up gain	Raises or lowers the compressed signal by a specified amount of dB

(Total 10 marks)

Question 12

Yes: 'Owner of a Lonely Heart' from *90125* (1983)   (4'29")

(a)   Which is the correct term for the repeated melodic idea heard through most of the song in the guitar
      and bass guitar?

      Lick ☒   Riff ☒   Fill ☒   Stab ☒   (1)

(b)   Which of the rhythms below best represents the rhythm of the figure described in question (a) in the
      section from 0'25"–0'40"?   (1)

(i) ☒

(ii) ☒

(iii) ☒

(iv) ☒

(c)   Describe the panning of the upwards glissando effect heard at 1'12"–1'13".

      .... (1)

(d)   The effect in the guitar solo from 2'32"–3'03" was created by recording a single guitar line (the lower
      line), pitch-shifting it and superimposing it onto the original track.

      (i) What is the interval between the two guitar lines?

      Perfect 5th ☒   Major 3rd ☒   Semitone ☒   Octave ☒   (1)

      (ii) When pitch-shifting a digital audio track, what adjustment would need to be made in order to
      preserve the tempo of the original track?

      .... (1)

(e)   Describe **three** changes in the texture in the passage from 1'57"–2'15" that contrast with the
      music of the preceding section.

      ....

      ....

      .... (3)

(f)   A Fairlight CMI was used in the making of this track and was an early example of a **sampler**.
      What is a sampler?

      ....

      .... (2)

(Total 10 marks)

AS level: section B questions

13. Special Focus Style: Rock 'n' Roll (examination years: 2009, 2013)

Little Richard: 'Lucille' from *Rock 'n' Roll Number 1s* (2007)   (2'32")

(a) This track shows many influences of **rhythm and blues**. Identify **three** features of rhythm and blues that can be heard on this track.

....

....

....   **(3)**

(b) Which of the following terms most closely describes the type of accompaniment from 1'00"–1'06"?

Stop time ☒   Turnaround ☒   Boogie woogie ☒   Bo Diddley beat ☒   **(1)**

(c) This recording contains a number of features that might be seen as shortcomings by today's standards. In the table below, identify **three** problems and suggest a way to solve the problem.   **(6)**

Aspect of recording	Description of problem	Possible solution
Stereo field	**Example:** the recording is in mono	**Example:** re-record the song using multi-track recording techniques, and pan the tracks to form an appropriate stereo image
Gain setting for vocals		
Clarity of individual instruments		
Balance between instruments		

(d) A precursor of rock 'n' roll in Britain was skiffle. Describe the distinguishing features of skiffle and assess its contribution to British popular music of the late 1950s and 1960s.

....

....

....

....

.... **(4)**

(e) Rock 'n' roll was the first form of popular music to achieve a mass popular appeal. Assess the role played by the following artists in the popularisation of rock 'n' roll:

(i) Bill Haley and The Comets

....

....

.... **(2)**

(ii) Elvis Presley

....

....

.... **(2)**

(iii) Cliff Richard

....

....

.... **(2)**

(Total 20 marks)

Sequencing exercise: sequence the vocal line of the first verse of 'Lucille', using pitch-bend to try to simulate the pitches Little Richard uses as accurately as possible. You may find it helpful to import the track as an audio file into your sequencing software for reference. For the very wide upward swoops, you may need to adjust the pitch-bend scaling, which is often found in the interface for the software instrument you are using.

Producing exercise: import a recent commercial recording of rock 'n' roll into a computer sequencer as an audio track. Remix it to replicate the general feel and recording quality of Little Richard's 'Lucille' that you identified in question (c) above. Experiment with EQ and panning, and explore your software's range of plug-ins (such as the 'Grungelizer' in Cubase) to produce the desired effect.

14. Special Focus Style: Hip hop (examination years: 2009, 2013)

Missy Elliott: 'Get Ur Freak On' from _Miss E ... So Addictive_ (2005) (3'31")

(a) Name the effect used on the spoken part that opens the track (0'00"–0'03").

.... **(1)**

(b) Rap and hip hop music is often notable for the creativity with which the main rap is delivered and broken up with vocal interjections of different sorts. Describe **four** different ways in which this song has used the human voice to bring variety and interest to the first verse section (from 0'26"–0'48").

(4)

Timing	Effect
0'28"	**Example:** backing vocals double rap on certain words and phrases to produce chorus effect
0'30"	**Example:** shouted exclamation on word 'Ah'
0'35"	
0'37"–0'40" and 0'45"–0'48"	
0'41"	
0'43"–0'44"	

(c) At 0'56", the phrase 'get ur' is repeated several times, imitating a common effect made possible by sampling technology and used extensively in club dance music. Which term most closely describes this effect?

Reverberating ☒   Retriggering ☒   Resampling ☒   Remixing ☒   **(1)**

(d) The section from 0'48"–1'09" can be thought of as a chorus section, contrasting with the music of the first verse. Name **four** ways in which the chorus contrasts with the verse. You may refer to instrumentation, texture, the material of the vocal line, melody, rhythm and harmony.

....

....

....

.... **(4)**

(e)   Briefly explain the following terms associated with rap and hip hop:

(i)   Toasting

....

....

....   **(2)**

(ii)   Breakdancing

....

....

....   **(2)**

(iii) Gangsta rap

....

....

....   **(2)**

(iv)   Grime

....

....

....   **(2)**

(v)   Breakbeat

....

....

....   **(2)**

(Total 20 marks)

Composing exercise: this track makes considerable use of ethnic percussion instruments and unusual rhythms. Using the rhythms in the song as a model, compose your own drum pattern using the ethnic percussion sounds available in your sequencing software.

15. Special Focus Style: Reggae (examination year: 2010)

Jacob Miller: 'Baby I Love You So' from *Songs for Reggae Lovers* (2008)   2'30"

Augustus Pablo: 'King Tubby Meets The Rockers Uptown' from *True Reggae* (2007)   2'32"

(a)   Identify the tempo in the Jacob Miller track.

    ♩= 52 ☒   ♩= 67 ☒   ♩= 90 ☒   ♩= 112 ☒   **(1)**

> **Hint:** using a watch or the time display on your playback device, count the number of beats there are in 30 seconds. Double this number to arrive at a fairly accurate approximation of the tempo.

(b)   Which wind instrument can be heard on the Jacob Miller track?

    Melodica ☒   Alto saxophone ☒   Muted trumpet ☒   Oboe ☒   **(1)**

> If you do not know the answer, eliminate instruments you are certain do not appear.

(c)   Compare the two tracks in the section from 0'00"– 1'00". In the table below, describe **four** ways in which Augustus Pablo's version of the track differs from Jacob Miller's version.'   **(8)**

	Changes in the Augustus Pablo version
Use of effects	**Example:** extensive use of reverb on the vocals (e.g. 0'09") and both reverb and delay on the guitar (e.g. 0'18")
Use of panning	
Use of dynamics	
Vocal part	
Drum kit part	

(d)   The Augustus Pablo track is a dub version of the Jacob Miller track. Identify **two** features of dub that can be heard on the Augustus Pablo track.

....

....   **(2)**

(e) Summarise the contribution made by **two** of the following groups to reggae. **(8)**

(i) The Skatalites

....

....

....

(ii) Bob Marley

....

....

....

(iii) The Specials

....

....

....

(Total 20 marks)

16. Special Focus Style: Heavy Rock (examination year: 2010)

Van Halen: 'Runnin' with the Devil' from *Van Halen* (1978) **(3'36")**

(a) The track opens with a recording of a car horn. Which of the following techniques has been used to alter this sound?

Modulation ☒   Flanging ☒   Pitch shifting ☒   Phasing ☒   **(1)**

(b) Describe how the musical arrangement reinforces the repeated notes of the bass line.

.... **(1)**

(c) Identify the guitar techniques used in the following places:

(i) 1'28"–1'29"

.... **(1)**

(ii) 1'43", 1'48", 1'53"

.... **(1)**

(iii) 2'27"–2'29"

.... **(1)**

(d) The lead guitarist on this track, Eddie Van Halen, was well known for a guitar technique known as **tapping**. Briefly describe what the technique of tapping involves and what sort of musical ideas it enables a guitarist to play.

....

.... **(2)**

(e) Describe **three** ways in which the vocal arrangement and performance creates the sense of macho, exhilarating abandon of the title of the track.

....

....

.... **(3)**

(f) Heavy rock makes extensive use of guitar distortion. Name **three** means by which guitar tone can be distorted.

....

....

.... **(3)**

(g) A common production technique associated with heavy rock makes creative use of the stereo field to make a guitar track sound 'fatter'. Name this technique and describe how it could be applied using modern technology.

....

....

.... **(2)**

(h) Describe what is meant by the term **'stadium rock'**.

....

....

.... **(2)**

(i) Assess the contribution of **one** of the following bands to heavy rock.

Led Zeppelin   Black Sabbath   Metallica

....

....

....

.... **(3)**

(Total 20 marks)

17. Special Focus Style: Soul (examination year: 2011)

The Temptations: 'My Girl' from *Motown 50* (2008) (2'57")

Otis Redding 'My Girl' (remastered mono album version) from *Otis Blue:* (2'56")
***Otis Redding Sings Soul* (2008)**

(a) Describe the differences between the features of the musical arrangement and production of the two versions of 'My Girl' listed in the table below. **(10)**

Feature	The Temptations	Otis Redding
Texture		
Instrumentation		
Separation between instruments		
Recording quality		
Ambience		

(b) The Temptations' version of 'My Girl' typifies Motown's 'wall of sound' technique.

   (i) Explain what is meant by this term.

....

....

.... **(2)**

   (ii) Describe the studio techniques that were originally used to create it.

....

....

.... **(2)**

(iii) How could a similar sound be achieved by using present-day recording techniques?

....

....

.... **(2)**

(c) Describe the contribution of **one** of the following artists or bands to soul, referring to at least one song in your answer.

Booker T and the MGs   Aretha Franklin   Marvin Gaye

....

....

....

....

.... **(4)**

(Total 20 marks)

18. Special Focus Style: Indie Rock (examination year: 2011)

The Smiths: 'That Joke isn't Funny Anymore' from *That Joke isn't Funny Anymore* (1985)   **(3'52")**

(a) Describe how the jangly acoustic guitar sound heard in the first 20 seconds of the track could be recreated using recording and mixing techniques.

....

....

.... **(2)**

(b) What is the time signature of the song?

$\frac{3}{4}$ ☒ $\frac{4}{4}$ ☒ $\frac{6}{8}$ ☒ $\frac{2}{4}$ ☒   **(1)**

(c) Describe the processing applied to the vocal track on the word 'laugh' at 0'38".

....

.... **(2)**

(d) The guitar track introduced at 1'05"–1'38" uses **autopan**. Describe how you would apply autopan to a track using an analogue mixing desk and using a computer sequencer.

Analogue mixing desk: ....

.... **(1)**

Computer sequencer: ....

.... **(1)**

(e)   The section from 1'54"–3'52" uses repetition to emphasise the words, but also contains subtle contrast to sustain the listener's interest. Describe **two** ways in which repetition and contrast have been used in this section.

Ways in which repetition has been used:

(i)   .... **(1)**

(ii) .... **(1)**

Ways in which variety has been introduced:

(i)   .... **(1)**

(ii) .... **(1)**

(f)   With which British city are The Smiths associated?

Liverpool ☒   Manchester ☒   London ☒   Sheffield ☒   **(1)**

(g)   This track was released in 1985, and contrasted strongly with the musical style, production and subject matter of commercial 1980s rock cultivated by major record labels. List **four** reasons why this song may not have initially appealed to a major record label at the time of its release from a commercial point of view.

....

....

....

.... **(4)**

(h)   Outline the contribution of **one** of the following to indie rock in Britain, referring to specific groups, albums or songs as appropriate to illustrate your argument.

The Fall   Factory Records   Radiohead

....

....

....

....

.... **(4)**

(Total 20 marks)

19. Special Focus Style: Punk and New Wave (examination year: 2012)

The Clash: 'Career Opportunities' from *The Essential Clash* (2003) (1'52")

(a) Is the song in a major or minor key?

.... (1)

(b) What is the effect used on the vocal track from 1'00"–1'14"?

.... (1)

(c) Describe **four** features of punk that can be heard on this track.

....

....

....

.... (4)

(d) In the table below, describe **two** problems that might occur when recording a punk vocalist and suggest how these could be overcome. (4)

Problem	Solution
Example: vocalist moving around during performance	**Example:** ask vocalist to stay the same distance away from microphone; set up a pop screen at an appropriate distance from the microphone and ask the vocalist to remain close to the pop screen

(e) The song details a list of uninspiring jobs that the singer was offered at a job centre. Why did the disaffected youth of the day turn to punk to voice their discontent rather than another style of popular music of the time, progressive rock?

Hint: for each reason you give, describe why punk was suitable and why progressive rock was unsuitable.

....

....

....

....

....

.... (6)

(f)   Describe the contribution to Punk or New Wave by **one** of the following artists.

     The Stooges   The Buzzcocks   Gary Numan

....

....

....

....

.... **(4)**

(Total 20 marks)

20. Special Focus Style: Club Dance (examination year: 2012)

Sash! and Stunt: 'Raindrops (Encore une fois) [Radio Edit]' from *Raindrops*   (2'58")
***(Encore une fois) [feat. Stunt]* (2008)**

(a)   Name the effect used on the voice at 0'39".

.... **(1)**

(b)   This track could be described as a 'mash-up'. What is meant by the term 'mash-up'?

....

.... **(2)**

(c)   Using a computer sequencer, how would you achieve the effect heard in the vocal track on the word 'alive' from 2'06"– 2'16"?

....

.... **(2)**

(d)   What structural term best describes the section from 2'06"– 2'23"?

.... **(1)**

(e)   Describe how the musical arrangement and production in the same section (2'06"– 2'23") creates a sense of building dramatically towards the re-entry of the kick drum at 2'23".

....

....

....

....

....

.... **(4)**

(f)   This track features several elements of **trance**. List **four** features of trance music that can be heard on this track.

....

....

....

.... **(4)**

> **Hint:** try to make your answer refer to features of trance rather than those of club dance music in general.

(g)   Trance differs from several other genres of club dance music in that it does not use samples of breakbeats. Name **two** sub-genres of dance music in which breakbeats are used.

....

.... **(2)**

(h)   Describe the contribution of **one** of the following to club dance music.

Norman Cook (Fatboy Slim)   Orbital   The Prodigy

....

....

....

....

....

.... **(4)**

(Total 20 marks)

A2 level

Introduction

The listening tests for A2-level Music Technology (Unit 4 Analysing and Producing) are worth 40% of the total A2 marks. The test takes the form of a single, two-hour examination sat in the summer term. The paper is made up of two sections: A and B, which have a total of 80 marks.

Section A consists of four questions and is worth a total of 62 marks (77.5% of Unit 4). Questions 1, 2 and 3 carry 46 marks in total, and to gain full marks in these questions you will need to submit **two audio files** that you will have processed, edited or compiled on your final submission audio CD. If the two audio files are not included as part of the final submission audio CD you will not gain any marks for questions relating to them.

Approximately half of the marks for section A questions will be practical (audio or MIDI processing for final audio CD submission) and half theoretical (written answers). Some of the questions in section A will require you to correct errors of pitch and rhythm on a staff notated score in relation to a recorded line. For these questions it is acceptable to make use of the MIDI keyboard of your DAW (digital audio workstation) to aid this process.

Question 4 will always be an essay style question (theoretical only) and will require you to write in detail about a piece of music technology or technological process. In the exam you will have a choice between two possible questions, but you only need to answer one, so choose the one with which you are most confident. Question 4 carries 16 marks in total, and to gain full marks you must include 16 different and relevant points. To gain good marks, it is essential to use the appropriate technical terms; so it is important to study how specific technology works and build up a vocabulary to describe this.

Section B is a practical only task and worth 18 marks (22.5% of Unit 4). You will be required to create a balanced stereo mix from the audio tracks that you have processed and imported into your DAW in section A. Marks for section B will be divided into six areas. Your ability to answer the six parts of question 5 will be solely judged by the **one further audio file** that you will add to your final submission audio CD. If this is not present you will gain no marks for section B.

Section B will be divided into the following areas of assessment, and each task will carry 3 marks:

> Managing and controlling EQ (Equalisation)
> Managing and controlling dynamics (Compression or similar)
> Effect/ambience (Reverb or similar)
> Use of stereo field (Pan, stereo delay, modulation effects or similar)
> Balance and blend (Mix)
> Mastering (Top and tail the file and normalize)

Your final submission audio CD: In total your final submission audio CD should contain three 16 bit 44.1kHz WAV files: two from section A and one from section B. The process of burning the final submission audio CD is **not** part of the examination. However, the audio files must be saved under exam conditions to a designated folder on the DAW exam computer. After the examination, the teacher or studio technician will burn your files to an audio CD and submit it to Edexcel.

General guidance for the exam

The exam audio files will be delivered via a CD-ROM from Edexcel in a similar format to the Rhinegold *Edexcel A2 Music Technology Listening Tests* CD that accompanies this study guide. The audio files must be loaded onto the local hard drive of your exam computer **before** the exam starts, as they will not be editable or run fast enough from the CD-ROM. Some sequencing packages do this automatically on import.

The main practical parts of this exam will require you to edit, mix and master a four-track song with the following or similar instruments:

1. Vocal or lead line
2. Piano or guitar, or other harmony or chordal instrument
3. Drums and/or percussion
4. Bass.

As you can see from the sample questions in this book, it is vital that you are quick and accurate at operating basic audio-editing and sequencer functions. You will be required to complete some of the following operations as part of the exam; it is important to practise these techniques so that you can complete them swiftly:

➤ Cutting, pasting and trimming
➤ Removing noise
➤ Adding/punching in and out effects
➤ Normalising
➤ Adjusting tempo
➤ Applying appropriate EQ, reverb, compression, chorus, delay and other effects
➤ Panning
➤ Pitch shifting
➤ Compiling a complete track from segments
➤ Editing or adding MIDI data in relation to a score or instructions including: lengthening notes, changing velocity, pitch or location, copying, looping, and quantising, to name a few.

Resources

It is important that your DAW is up to task, with modern sequencing software and plugin set (Logic or Cubase for example), a MIDI keyboard, headphones and a CD drive capable of reading and writing discs. The DAW should be able to keep up with the speed at which you work and not slow you down.

Sample Paper 1

Time: 2 hours
Pop/Funk – 'Sorry'. Words and music Alec Boulton ©

Section A
Instructions for Section A

Open your DAW (digital audio workstation) and create a new project with:

- Three stereo audio tracks
- One MIDI track
- Set sequencer bpm to 110 with a time signature of $\frac{4}{4}$
- Change the time signature at bars 10 and 19 only to $\frac{2}{4}$, all other bars should be $\frac{4}{4}$.

> This might happen automatically when opening or importing the MIDI file depending on your sequencer. But if not, change the barlines manually. Although you are not marked on this, it will be difficult to follow the tables below if you have not changed the time signature.

- Open the folder 'SP1 Sorry' from the *Edexcel A2 Music Technology Listening Tests* CD.

> This CD is available for purchase from Rhinegold Education, ISBN: 978-1-906178-91-8.

- The folder contains nine audio files and one MIDI file that form the end of the song 'Sorry' from the musical *The Unseen* © Word Action Productions Ltd.

Question 1 (12 marks)

Select a MIDI track and 'import' the file 'Sorry 02 electric piano.mid' onto it. The file should start at bar 1; the first notes should sound on beat 2 of bar 1.

(a) Assign an electric piano to the MIDI part. **(2)**

(b) This was originally played live in two parts: the changeover happens in bar 11 where the pianist starts using the pedal. The pedal blurs the upper notes. Remove all sustain controls from the MIDI part (control 64). **(2)**

(c) What is control number 10?

   Sostenuto ☒   Pan ☒   Breath controller ☒   Balance ☒   Portamento ☒ **(1)**

(d) Modulation is a continuous controller, unlike a note on or note off instruction. In the table below, write in the 'data 1' and 'data 2' columns the values to instruct a typical sequencer to achieve a modulation of 50% of the maximum. In the 'range of values' column, enter the maximum number of possible steps of this controller.

	Data 1	Data 2	Range of values
Controller			
	(1)	(1)	(1)

(3)

(e)   There are three incorrect notes in the MIDI track.

   (i)   Delete the F♯ in bar 9.   **(1)**

   (ii)   Change the B in bar 12 to a B♭.   **(1)**

   (iii)   Lengthen the four lowest quaver notes (⅛ notes) (D, A♭, C and D) at bar 17, halfway through beat 2, by an additional minim (½ note). The original extract looks like this on the note editor:

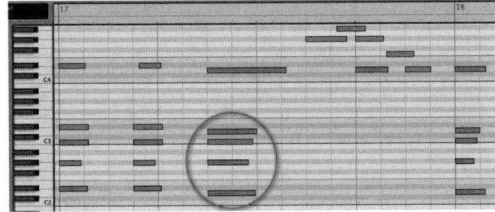

                                                                                                 (1)

   (iv)   Add a new quaver F, a minor 3rd below the last A♭ in bar 28 beat 3, at full velocity to complete the electric piano part.   **(1)**

Solo the completed electric piano part.

Bounce/export the completed electric piano part as a **single** 16 bit/44.1 kHz stereo WAV file to the designated folder on your computer.

Name it 'Sorry TK1_[your candidate number]'.

                                                                              (Total 12 marks)

Question 2 (18 marks)

Import WAV files ('Sorry 03–09 drums.wav') to one empty stereo audio track.

(a) Using the table below compile a single continuous drum track: (6)

Bar	Track
1	Sorry 03 drums.wav
2–3	Sorry 04 drums.wav
4–5	Sorry 04 drums.wav
6–7	Sorry 04 drums.wav
8–9	Sorry 04 drums.wav
10 ($\frac{2}{4}$ bar)	Sorry 04 drums.wav – cut end of file so as to fit into bar 10 which is a $\frac{2}{4}$ bar
11	Sorry 05 drums.wav
12–13	Sorry 06 drums.wav
14–15	Sorry 06 drums.wav
16–17	Sorry 06 drums.wav
18	Sorry 06 drums.wav – cut end of file so it fits into bar 18
19 ($\frac{2}{4}$ bar)	Sorry 07 drums.wav in $\frac{2}{4}$ bar
20	Sorry 05 drums.wav
21–22	Sorry 08 drums.wav
23–end	Sorry 09 drums.wav

(b) Describe what a compressor does. Refer to the following specific controls and link ratio, attack and release to the threshold:

(i) Compressor (general definition)

....

.... (2)

(ii) Threshold

....

.... (2)

(iii) Ratio

....

.... (2)

(iv) Attack

....

.... (2)

(v) Release

....

.... (2)

(vi)   Gain

....

.... (2)

Solo the completed drum/percussion part.

Bounce/export the completed drum/percussion track as a **single** 16 bit/44.1 kHz stereo WAV file to the designated folder on your computer.

Name it 'Sorry TK2_[your candidate number]'.

(Total 18 marks)

Question 3 (16 marks)

Import 'Sorry 01 vox.wav.' of the CD-ROM to a new stereo audio track. This track is a complete vocal part. Ensure that the beginning of this audio track is aligned with the start of bar 1. The vocal begins playing in bar 9.

(a) Play the track while following the score. In the main vocal there are three errors in the score where the pitch does not match the audio file. Identify **two** errors by circling them and placing 'ai' and 'aii' above the stave of each.   **(2)**

On the staves below rewrite each bar in full with the correct pitch; include a time signature. You do **not** need to write out the lyrics.

(i)   (ii)

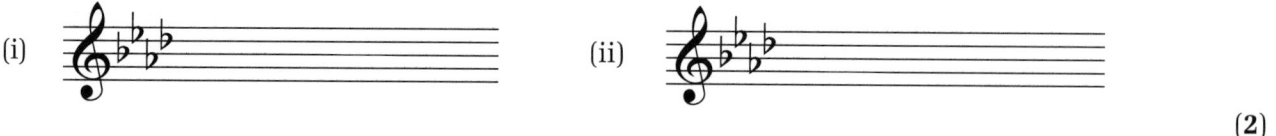

(2)

(b) The score also contains two rhythmic errors. Identify the errors by circling them and placing 'bi' and 'bii' above the stave of each.   **(2)**

On the staves below rewrite each bar in full with the correct pitch; include a time signature. You do **not** need to write out the lyrics.

(i)   (ii)

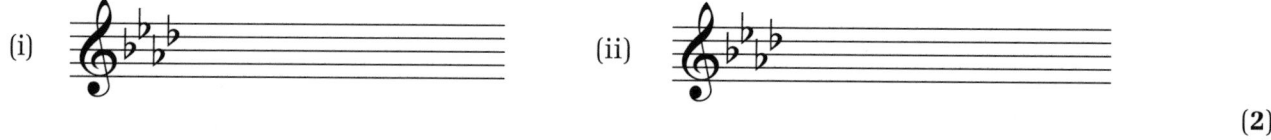

(2)

(c) This track was recorded in four takes after the instrumental tracks. What is this process called?

....   **(2)**

(d) This track was recorded using a large diaphragm condenser microphone with a cardioid pick-up pattern. A polar pattern is a 2-D representation of this.

(i)   Draw the shape of a cardioid polar pattern on the diagram below.   **(2)**

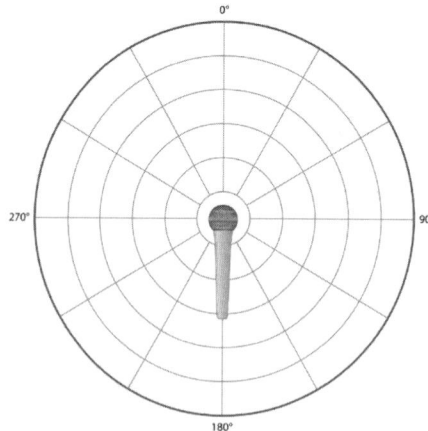

(ii) Place a D on your polar pattern where it is **most** sensitive to sound.   **(1)**

(iii) Place an X on your polar pattern where it is **least** sensitive to sound.   **(1)**

(iv) Name another polar pattern.

....   **(2)**

(Total 16 marks)

Sorry

Alec Boulton

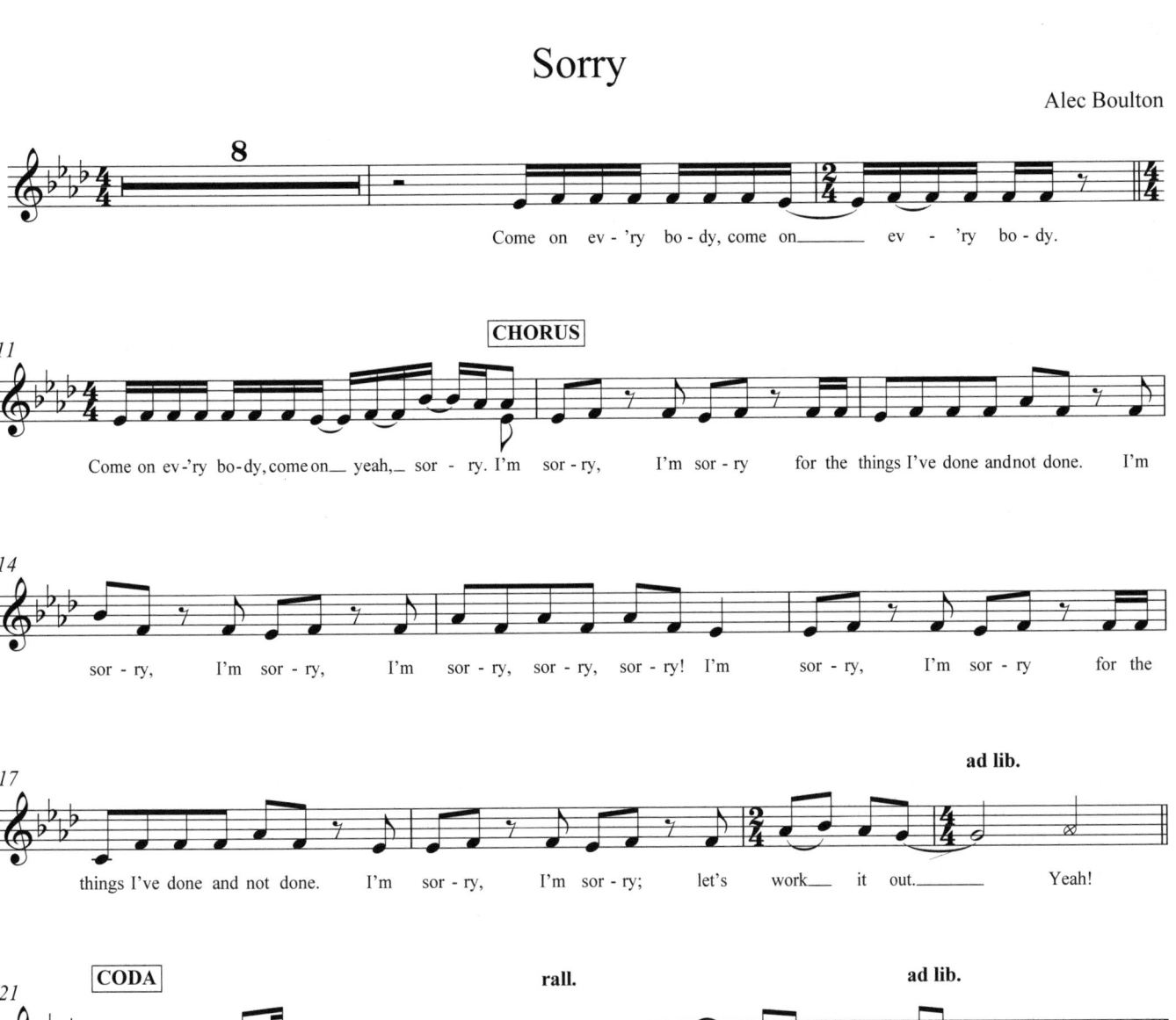

Question 4 (16 marks)

Analogue tape was not the only recordable media when it was first introduced. However, it was the first to offer high-quality recordings that could be edited and did not significantly degrade in quality from one play to the next. Describe how analogue tape and the tape recorder function, using technical terminology.

You are advised to keep your answer to around 200 words. You may write in continuous prose, bullet points or use a table to communicate your answer.

> In the actual Edexcel A2 exam you will be able to choose from one of two questions to answer, but only one has been given here. You will have two pages of blank lines on which to write your answer – we are unable to reproduce these here for space reasons.

Section B

Question 5 (18 marks)

You should now have the following tracks on your computer:

- 'Sorry TK1_your candidate number' (electric piano)
- 'Sorry TK2_your candidate number' (drums)
- 'Sorry 01 vox.wav' (vocal)
- 'Sorry 10 bass.wav' (bass) – import this now onto the next available audio track, you will need to line the first bass note attack/pluck with the first beat of bar 1.

Produce a balanced stereo mix following the instructions below.

(a) Compress the vocal track.

- The settings should bring out the detail in the quieter parts of the voice
- Do not over-compress the vocal. **(3)**

(b) Add an EQ to the bass line.

- Make the bass line sound rich and full – it is too weak at the moment
- Do not allow the bass to boom. **(3)**

(c) Add a stereo-delay to the last few notes of the electric piano.

- Set up a stereo multi-tap delay effect that continues sounding slightly after the final cymbal crash and gradually fades away
- The settings should swing/groove to the music
- Do not add too much feedback. **(3)**

(d) Apply reverb to each of the four tracks.

- 1.5 second reverb time
- The reverb should be subtle
- The electric piano should have the most reverb, followed by the vocal and drums; the bass should have very little. **(3)**

(e) Balance the mix

- The balance should suit the style of pop/funk music
- The electric piano may require automation when the vocal line enters
- Each track should be clearly heard. **(3)**

(f) Produce a final stereo mix.

- Ensure the mix output is at a strong level
- It should be free from distortion/clipping
- Do not limit or compress the final mix output
- Do not cut off the reverb tail or electric piano delay
- Include a short audio silence (approximately 0.5 seconds) at the beginning and end of the mix. **(3)**

(Total 18 marks)

Bounce/export the completed mix as a <u>single</u> 16 bit, 44.1kHz stereo .wav file to the designated folder on your computer.

Name it 'Sorry TK3_[your candidate number]'.

Sample Paper 2

Time: 2 hours
Retro Pop – 'Holler'. Words and music BillyBottle © 2007 (extract)

Section A
Instructions for Section A

Open your DAW (digital audio workstation) and create a new project with:

- Four stereo audio tracks
- Set the sequencer bpm to 81 with a time signature of $\frac{4}{4}$.

Open the folder 'SP2 Holler' from the *Edexcel A2 Music Technology Listening Tests* CD. The folder contains ten audio files that form an extract of the song 'Holler'.

Question 1 (14 marks)

Import 'Holler 10 vox.wav' from the CD-ROM to a new **stereo** audio track in your music production software. This track is a complete vocal part. Ensure that the beginning of this audio track is aligned with the start of bar 1. The vocal begins playing in bar 3 just before beat 4.

Import 'Holler 01 piano.wav' from the CD-ROM to a new **stereo** audio track in your music production software. This track is a complete piano part. Ensure that the beginning of this audio track is aligned with the start of bar 1. The piano begins playing straight away at bar 1 beat 1.

(a) Play the vocal track while following the score (overleaf). In the vocal line there are three errors in the score where the pitch does not match the audio file. Identify **two** of the errors by circling them and placing 'ai' and 'aii' above the stave of each. **(2)**

On the staves below rewrite each bar in full to reflect the correct pitch of the audio file. You do **not** need to write out the lyrics.

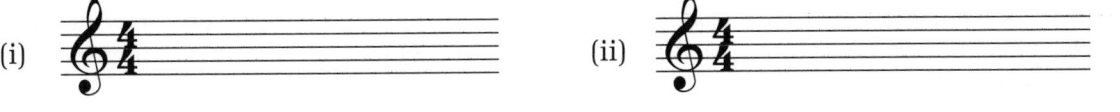

(i)   (ii)

(2)

(b) The score also contains two rhythmic errors. Identify the errors by circling them and placing 'bi' and 'bii' above the stave of each. **(2)**

On the staves below rewrite the full bar using the correct note values and where necessary, rests. You do **not** need to write out the lyrics.

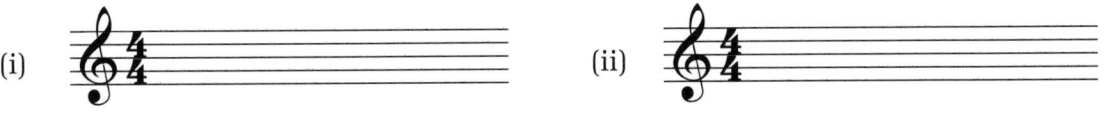

(i)   (ii)

(2)

Holler

Billy Bottle

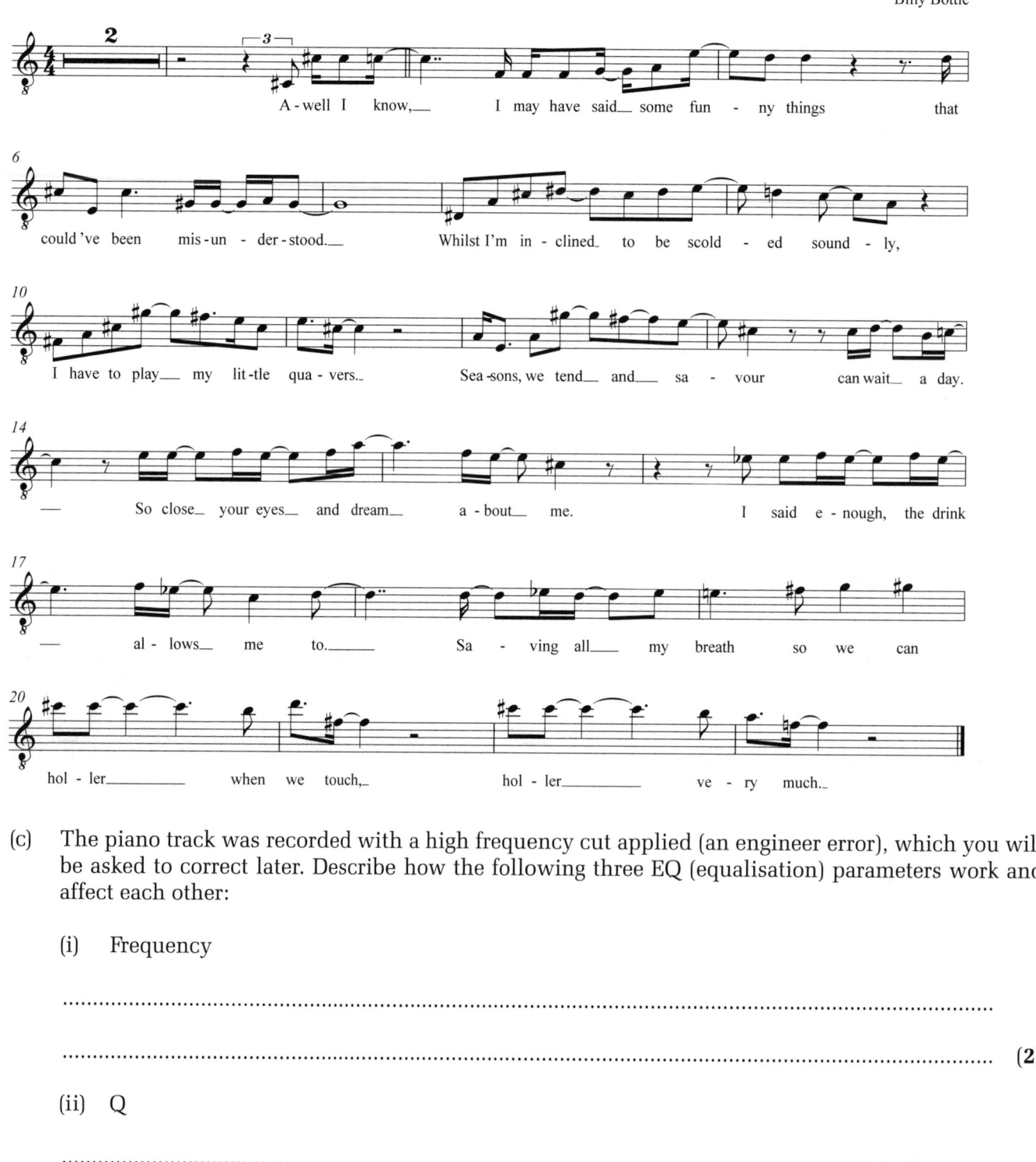

(c) The piano track was recorded with a high frequency cut applied (an engineer error), which you will be asked to correct later. Describe how the following three EQ (equalisation) parameters work and affect each other:

(i) Frequency

....

.... **(2)**

(ii) Q

....

.... **(2)**

(iii) Gain

....

.... **(2)**

(Total 14 marks)

Question 2 (18 marks)

Import the WAV files shown in the table below ('Holler 02 bass.wav', 'Holler 03 bass.wav', 'Holler 04 bass.wav') to a stereo audio track. Using the table below, compile a single bass track with all operations/corrections made.

	File name	Bar number	Operation
(a)	Holler 02 bass.wav	1–7	Fade out the long held bass note so as to not clash with the harmony (3)
(b)	Holler 03 bass.wav	13–end	Put in the correct location and cut from bar 23 just before beat 3 (3)
(c)	Holler 04 bass.wav	23–end	Adjust the gain to match the volume of the bass line in bar 22 (4)
(d)	Holler 04 bass.wav	23–end	Create a seamless fast cross-fade at an appropriate point at the start of bar 23 so that file 'Holler 03 bass.wav' fades out to be replaced with 'Holler 04 bass.wav'. No glitches should be heard. (4)

(e) The synthesiser bass line was recorded direct from its line outputs into a line level mixing desk input. What is the difference between line level input and microphone level input?

(i) Microphone:

....

.... (2)

(ii) Line:

....

.... (2)

Solo the completed bass part.

Bounce/export the completed bass part as a **single** 16-bit, 44.1 kHz stereo WAV file to the designated folder on your computer.

Name it 'Holler TK1_[your candidate number]'.

(Total 18 marks)

Question 3 (14 marks)

Import the WAV files shown in the table below to one empty stereo audio track. Using the table below, compile a single drum track. Please note that there will be some silence during the verse.

File name	Bar number	Operation
(a) Holler 05 drums	2–5	Put in correct location (1)
(b) Holler 06 drums	13–14	Put in correct location (1)
(c) Holler 07 drums	15	Loop until end of bar 18 (3)
(d) Holler 08 drums	19	Top and tail Holler 08 drums.wav to fit into bar 19 only. You will need to cut one bar off the start and one off the end of the file; both guiro sounds should be cut (3)
(e) Holler 09 drums	20–25	Put in correct location (1)

The table below is a MIDI representation of the kick, snare and cymbal sounds of the first bar of the drums. The start and end times for each event are given as follows: bars.crotchets.semiquavers.ticks (1.1.1.1)

Start	Status	Channel	Data 1	Data 2	End
1.1.1.1	Program	10	–	0	–
1.1.1.1	Controller	10	7 (volume)	100	–
1.1.1.1	Controller	10	10 (pan)	127	–
2.1.1.1	Note (Ride Bell)	10	F2	54	2.1.2.240
2.1.1.16	Note (Kick 2)	10	B0	98	2.1.2.36
2.1.2.232	Note (Kick 2)	10	B0	47	2.1.4.12
2.2.1.1	Note (Snare 1)	10	D1	119	2.2.2.1
2.2.1.1	Note (Snare 2)	10	E1	119	2.2.2.1
2.2.1.1	Note (Ride 1)	10	D#2	54	2.2.3.1
2.2.4.1	Note (Kick 2)	10	B0	46	2.2.4.240
2.3.1.1	Note (Kick 2)	10	B0	86	2.3.3.1
2.4.1.1	Note (Snare 1)	10	D1	119	2.4.2.67
2.4.1.1	Note (Snare 2)	10	E1	119	2.4.2.67
2.4.1.1	Note (Ride 1)	10	D#2	98	2.4.2.238

(f)   What is the velocity of the first note in the above sequence?

....
(1)

(g)   Which part of the drum kit is not fully quantised to quavers?

....
(1)

(h)   What is the main volume of the drum channel?

....
(1)

(i)   This track will not play back in a similar way to the audio drum track. What is the panning error and how could it be corrected?

Mistake:

.... **(1)**

Correction:

.... **(1)**

> Solo the completed drum part.
>
> Bounce/export the completed bass part as a **single** 16-bit, 44.1 kHz stereo WAV file to the designated folder on your computer.
>
> Name it 'Holler TK2_[your candidate number]'.

(Total 14 marks)

Question 4 (16 marks)

By the early 1980s, digital synthesisers had almost completely replaced their analogue equivalents. However, a digital synthesiser's functionality, control and sound are borrowed almost exclusively from its analogue counterpart of the 1960s–1970s. Describe how an analogue subtractive synthesiser functions and is controlled, using technical terminology.

You are advised to keep your answer to around 200 words. You may write in continuous prose, bullet points or use a table to communicate your answer.

> In the actual Edexcel A2 exam you will be able to choose from one of two questions to answer, but only one has been given here. You will have two pages of blank lines on which to write your answer – we are unable to reproduce these here for space reasons.

Section B

Question 5 (18 marks)

You should now have the following tracks on your computer:

- 'Holler 10 vox.wav' (vocal)
- 'Holler 01 piano.wav' (piano)
- 'Holler TK1_your candidate number' (bass)
- 'Holler TK2_your candidate number' (drums).

Produce a balanced stereo mix following the instructions below:

(a)   Add an EQ to the piano line.

- The upper and mid frequencies are muffled: correct this error
- The tone should be natural.   (**3**)

(b)   Compress the vocal line.

- The vocal line has a range of different dynamics, set the threshold to even it out
- Do not over-compress.   (**3**)

(c)   Automate a stereo pan at bar 13 on the first two hits of the drum track (bass drum, then snare).

- The pan should not move during each drum attack, but just after
- Pan the first hit left and the second hit right, but do not pan fully left or right
- Return the drum track to centre pan position after the second hit.   (**3**)

(d)   Apply reverb to each of the four tracks.

- Use a reverb time approximately 1 sec
- The reverb should be subtle but add presence
- The piano should have the most reverb, followed by less on the vocal and drums; the bass should have very little.   (**3**)

(e)   Balance the mix.

- The balance should suit the style of pop-rock music
- The vocal may require automation entering the chorus from bar 19
- Each track should be clearly heard.   (**3**)

(f)   Produce a final stereo mix.

- Ensure the mix output is at a high level
- It should be free from distortion/clipping
- Do not limit or compress the final mix output
- Do not cut off the reverb tail
- Include a short audio silence (approximately 0.5 seconds) at the beginning and end of the mix. (**3**)

Bounce/export the completed mix as a **single** 16-bit, 44.1 kHz stereo WAV file to the designated folder on your computer.

Name it 'Holler TK3_[your candidate number]'.

(**Total 18 marks**)

Sample Paper 3

Time: 2 hours
Jazz standard – 'I Won't Tell Mercutio'. Words and music Alec Boulton © 2001 (extract)

Section A
Instructions for Section A

Open your DAW (digital audio workstation) and create a new project with:

- Three stereo audio tracks and one mono audio track (for the bass line)
- Set sequencer bpm to 88 with a time signature of $\frac{4}{4}$.

Open the folder 'SP3 Mercutio' from the *Edexcel A2 Music Technology Listening Tests* CD. The folder contains six audio tracks that form the start of the song 'I Won't Tell Mercutio'.

Question 1 (19 marks)

Select a stereo audio track and import the file 'Mercutio 01 vox.wav' onto the track. Ensure that the beginning of the file is aligned with the start of bar 1. The vocal begins playing at bar 6.

The vocal was recorded in a number of different takes and the best takes cross-faded (x-faded) together. A few errors still exist that you will correct. Follow the instructions in the table below:

	File name	Bar number	Operation
(a)	Mercutio 01 vox.wav	21 start of bar	Adjust the gain of the words 'I love' to match the volume of the surrounding audio **(4)**
(b)	Mercutio 01 vox.wav	23–end	Pitch-shift the vocal line, final 'I love you' from bar 23, up one semitone (+100 cents) so that it is in harmony with rest of the song **(4)**

(c)   This track was originally recorded with a male bass voice and microphone placement that resulted in considerable proximity effect. What is the proximity effect?

....

....

.... **(3)**

(d)   Play the vocal track while following the score (overleaf). In the main vocal there are three errors in the score, bars 1–22, where the pitch does not match the audio file. Identify **two** errors by circling them and placing 'di' and 'dii' above the stave of each. **(2)**

On the staves below rewrite each bar in full with the correct pitch; include a time signature. You do **not** need to write out the lyrics.

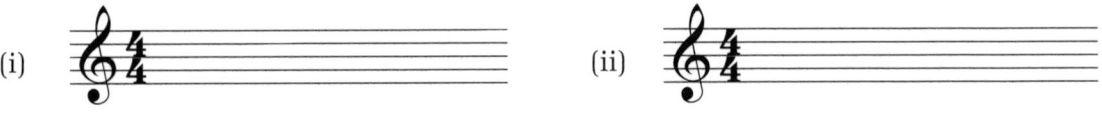

(2)

I won't tell Mercutio

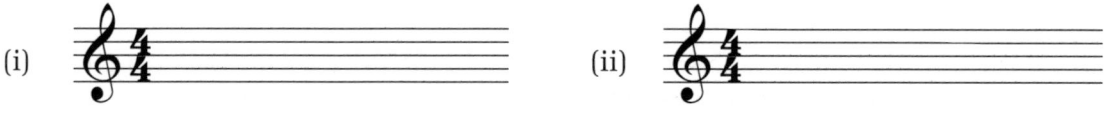

(e) The score also contains two rhythmic errors. Identify the errors by circling them and placing 'ei' and 'eii' above the stave of each. **(2)**

On the staves below rewrite the full bar using the correct note values and where necessary, rests. You do **not** need to write out the lyrics.

(i)   (ii)

(2)

> Solo the completed vocal part.
>
> Bounce/export the completed vocal part as a **single** 16-bit, 44.1 kHz stereo WAV file to the designated folder on your computer.
>
> Name it 'Mercutio TK1_[your candidate number]'.

(Total 19 marks)

Question 2 (18 marks)

Import the WAV file 'Mercutio 02 guitar main.wav' onto a stereo audio track so the music begins playing from bar 1. Then import the files 'Mercutio 03 gt start replacement.wav' and

'Mercutio 04 gt end replacement.wav' to the same track and, using the table below, compile a single continuous guitar track with all operations/corrections made.

File name	Bar number	Operation
(a) Mercutio 02 guitar main.wav	16, beat 4	Remove the mistake notes at given location (4)
(b) Mercutio 03 gt start replacement.wav	1–7	Position and cross-fade. This file needs to replace 'Mercutio 01 Guitar Main.wav' from bars 1–5 inclusive. The chord at the start of bar 6 should be from file 'Mercutio 01 Guitar Main.wav' (4)
(c) Mercutio 04 gt end replacement.wav	22–26	Position and cross-fade. This file needs to replace 'Mercutio 01 Guitar Main.wav' from bars 22–26, but should only sound a fraction before bar 23 then continue to the end. (4)

(d) The guitar in this track is electro-acoustic and was recorded with a single condenser microphone. Other than with a microphone, what method of capturing this guitar would be best used in a live situation?

.... **(1)**

(e) How would the recorded room ambience be affected by the capturing technique in (d)?

.... **(1)**

> Solo the completed guitar part.
>
> Bounce/export the completed guitar part as a **single** 16-bit, 44.1 kHz stereo WAV file to the designated folder on your computer.
>
> Name it 'Mercutio TK2_[your candidate number]'.

The table below is a MIDI representation of the notes of the guitar part at the same bars. The start and end times for each event are given as follows: bars.crotchets.semiquavers.ticks (1.1.1.1). The 'info' part of the column only refers to pitch-bend data entries.

Start	Status	Channel	Data 1	Data 2	End/Info
1.1.1.1	Program	1	–	88	–
1.1.1.1	Controller	1	93	127	–
1.1.1.1	Controller	1	7	100	–
1.1.1.1	Pitch-bend	1	0	64	0
11.3.2.193	Note	1	F2	52	11.4.2.2
11.3.3.109	Note	1	C3	43	11.4.2.2
11.3.3.206	Note	1	E3	40	11.4.2.2
11.3.4.157	Note	1	A3	56	11.4.2.2
15.2.4.45	Note	1	A3	45	15.3.3.1
15.2.4.45	Note	1	D4	45	15.3.3.1
15.2.4.121	Pitch-bend	1	0	96	4096
15.3.1.1	Pitch-bend	1	127	127	8191
16.1.2.55	Note	1	G2	78	16.1.3.70
16.1.2.55	Note	1	D3	72	16.1.3.70
16.1.2.55	Note	1	A3	84	16.1.3.70
16.1.2.56	Pitch-bend	1	0	64	0

(f)   Name the two guitar techniques the programmer is trying to emulate at:

Bar 11

.... **(1)**

Bar 15

.... **(1)**

(g)   The programmer has failed to clear the pitch bend before the chord beginning at 16.1.2.55. Given a default pitch-bend range, how will the chord at bar 16 sound incorrectly?

.... **(1)**

(h)   What is the velocity of the first note of bar 15?

.... **(1)**

(Total 18 marks)

Question 3 (9 marks)

Import 'Mercutio 06 drums.wav' of the CD-ROM to a new stereo audio track in your music production software. This track is a complete drum part. Ensure that the beginning of this audio track is aligned with the start of bar 1. The drums begin playing at bar 2 beat 1.

(a)   Import the file 'Mercutio 05 bass.wav' of the CD-ROM to a new **mono** audio track in your music production software. The bass begins playing at bar 2 beat 1. Edit the file following the 'operation' instructions in the table below.

File name	Bar number	Operation
Mercutio 05 bass.wav	1–end	Cut or fade out the unwanted noise at the end of the file (creaking floor, ambient movement noises) **(4)** This will be assessed on the final master mix only. If no final mix is present, you will score 0 marks (you do not need to burn a separate bass file).

(b)   Like the vocal and guitar lines, the bass line was recorded in a few takes with the best takes cross-faded together. How does a cross-fade (x-fade) work?

....

....

.... **(3)**

(c)   The drum track, unlike the bass line, was programmed using multi-velocity (multi-strike) samples for the snare drum and other brush strokes. What is multi-velocity sampling?

....

.... **(2)**

(Total 9 marks)

Question 4 (16 marks)

During the late 1990s to early 2000s, digital hard disc recording rapidly surpassed analogue tape as the preferred tracking format. The technology at the heart of this revolution was the A/D (analogue-to-digital) converter and the hard drive or hard disc. Using technical terminology, describe an A/D converter and how it works.

You are advised to keep your answer to around 200 words. You may write in continuous prose, bullet points or use a table to communicate your answer.

> In the actual Edexcel A2 exam you will be able to choose from one of two questions to answer, but only one has been given here. You will have two pages of blank lines on which to write your answer – we are unable to reproduce these here for space reasons.

Section B

Question 5 (18 marks)

You should now have the following tracks on your computer:

- 'Mercutio TK1_your candidate number' (vocal)
- 'Mercutio TK2_your candidate number' (guitar)
- 'Mercutio 05 bass.wav' (bass)
- 'Mercutio 06 drums.wav' (drums).

Produce a balanced stereo mix following the instructions below:

(a)   Add an EQ to the drum track.

- The mid-to-high frequencies sound too muffled: correct this
- Do not allow the bass drum to boom.   **(3)**

(b)   Compress the vocal line.

- Use a setting that allows all the words to be heard clearly and places the vocal forward in the mix
- Do not over-compress the vocals or make them sound unnatural.   **(3)**

(c)   Add a stereo-delay plugin to the guitar from the start to the first chord of bar 5.

- Assign a delay offset of approximately 700ms left and 1300ms right
- Delay at the crotchet for left and minim for right
- Keep the feedback low.   **(3)**

(d)   Apply reverb to each of the four tracks.

- One-second reverb time
- The reverb should be smooth and warm but not overpowering
- The vocal should have the most reverb, with less on the guitar, slightly less still on the drums and only a small amount on the bass.   **(3)**

(e)   Balance the mix.

- The balance should suit the jazz music style
- Each track should be clearly heard
- The vocal should be slightly more prominent.   **(3)**

(f)   Produce a final stereo mix.

- Ensure the mix output is at a high level
- It should be free from distortion/clipping
- Do not limit or compress the final mix output
- Do not cut off the reverb tail
- Include a short audio silence (approximately 0.5 seconds) at the beginning and end of the mix. **(3)**

Bounce/export the completed mix as a **single** 16-bit, 44.1 kHz stereo WAV file to the designated folder on your computer.

Name it 'Mercutio TK3_[your candidate number]'.

(Total 18 marks)

Answers

The answers given here are intended as a guide. Alternative answers will always receive credit if they form an accurate and unambigious response to the question.

Section A questions

Question 1
Mudhoney: 'Let it Slide'

(a)   Black Sabbath

(b)   Any **two** of: muddy, unfocused, 'dirty' sound, rich in dissonant overtones; use of fuzz; use of distortion; use of feedback.

(c)   Feedback

(d)   Use of call and response (**1**), and the guitar's version is different (**1**). (The lead guitar loosely imitates the rhythm and shape of the vocal line using the device of call and response. The guitar's material is an elaborated version of that of the vocal line, using slides and moving upwards instead of downwards.)

(e)   Octaves

(f)   Any **two** of: record using a simple set-up of two overheads, and close mics on the snare and kick drum (**1**); place stereo overhead microphones at about 1.5–2 metres above the kit to pick up a mix of direct sound and room ambience, creating an impression of depth – this also reduces the separation between the individual instruments in the kit (**1**); record in a 'live' room with reflective surfaces to create reverberation/room ambience (**1**).

(g)   As the guitar tone in grunge is generally very muddy, guitars can mask each other. Separating them in the stereo field enables the individual guitars to be distinguished more clearly.

Question 2
The Beach Boys: 'I Get Around'

(a)   Falsetto

(b)   (iii)

(c)

Timing	Change in instrumentation
0'20"	**Example:** lead vocal accompanied by bass
0'24"	**Example:** as above, but with clapping on each beat introduced
0'27"	Lead guitar lick; hi-hat on semiquavers; organ chord
0'30"	Lead vocal accompanied by bass, with guitar doubling bass line
0'33"	As above, with clapping on each beat introduced
0'37"	Lead vocal, accompanied by b.vox, rhythm guitar, kit and bass

(d)   Doo-wop

(e)   (i)   Arrange the singers in a semicircle around the microphone, so that each singer is equidistant from it. The exact distance away for each singer is governed by how loud each singer is: a loud singer would need to be further away to ensure equal balance.

       (ii)   The disadvantages are that there is no stereo field (**1**); the relative level/EQ/depth of individual voices cannot be altered in the mix (**1**); and differences in tone between the voices may be produced by off-axis coloration (**1**). (2 marks total)

Question 3
Isaac Hayes: 'Theme from Shaft'

(a)   Wah-wah pedal/wah pedal

(b)

Rhythm guitar	Trumpet	Organ	Hi-hat/ride cymbal

Bass/Keyboard	Flute	Trombone	Guitar (chords)

(c)   (iv)

(d)   It is panned continuously across the stereo field.

(e)   Any two of: very tight, rhythmic playing; heavily syncopated rhythms; use of muted guitar chords; jazz-influenced harmonies, such as 7th and 9th chords; use of horn section stabs; use of speaking/ shouting and vocalisations delivered in a sexually charged manner.

(f)   Any one of: record the percussion track in real time and sequence the other parts using this as a guide; sequence the track in step time and use a tempo track to mirror the tempo changes; create a tempo map and sequence each part using the tempo map as a guide.

Question 4
Tammy Wynette: 'The Ways to Love a Man'

(a) $\frac{12}{8}$

(b)   Hawaiian guitar (or lap steel guitar, lap slide guitar, pedal steel guitar)

(c)   Db, Ab, Eb, C

(d)   Volume

(e)   Country

(f)   Any **two** of: introduction of backing vocals providing a chordal backing (**1**); lead vocals are louder and in a higher register (**1**); acoustic guitar's accompaniment pattern becomes fuller (**1**), with strummed chords in a repeated crotchet-quaver rhythm (**1**); change from rim click to snare played with brush on beats 2 and 4 (**1**); unexpected chord change (use of a C major chord in A flat major) (**1**)

Question 5
Queen: 'Killer Queen'

(a)   Flanging (or phasing)

(b)

Start time	End time	How the stereo field is used
1'22"	1'26"	**Example:** backing vocals on the phrases 'bah bah bah bah' and 'anytime' are panned respectively hard left and hard right
1'49"	2'02"	Three different overdubbed guitar tracks are clearly differentiated from one another by the use of panning: one is panned hard left, another centrally and the third hard right (**3**)
2'11"	2'17"	The lead guitar moves in the stereo field from left to right (**2**); the backing vocals on the phrases 'drive you wild' and 'wild' are panned respectively hard right and hard left (**2**) (2 marks total)

(c)   Use a stereo pair of condenser microphones and, with the lid of the piano open, place them just inside the case pointing downwards and slightly inwards towards the middle of the instrument, one next to the lower strings and one next to the higher strings.

(d) $\frac{4}{4}$

(e)   Roll

Question 6
Eurythmics: 'Who's That Girl'

(a)

(b)   The second passage has a shorter reverberation time than the first; the first passage uses reverb, the second gated reverb

(c)

Timing	Description of vocal arrangement	Production/mixing techniques used
0'37"–0'39"	**Example:** a second vocal part is added, which shadows the contour of the melody, and adding harmonies	**Example:** the capture is similar to that of the lead vocal, but it is set back in the mix slightly; it is panned slightly to the left.
0'52"–1'02"	A homophonic idea is used on the setting 'But there's just one thing'	The voices are panned around the centre of the stereo field; a delay effect is used; gated reverb is used
0'53"–0'55"	A breathy noise is added	Use of reverb
0'58"–1'09"	A wordless melismatic/heavily ornamented soulful vocal solo line is added	It is set further back in the mix through the use of more reverb, and panned slightly to the right

Question 7
Jimi Hendrix: 'Purple Haze'

(a)   Pedal note. This is a tonic pedal, meaning it is the note of the home key of the song.

(b)   Divebomb

(c)

Timing	Instrument	Production Feature
1'37–1'53"	'Ooh' and 'ah' sounds	EQ of the 'ooh', 'aah' breath noises enhances aspirate sounds (1); reverb applied (1); two similar versions of the noises are sounded simultaneously and panned to hard left and hard right (1)
2'36"–2'50"	Guitar tremolo note	The note is panned back and forth across the stereo field (1)

Timing	Feature	Description
1'13"–1'36"	Melody	Expressive, improvisatory guitar solos (1), covering a wide range (1)
2'23"–2'50"	Texture	Thick improvisatory texture (1); frenetic improvisation (1) and extended techniques (1) in the guitar parts; use of extreme high guitar register (1)

(d)   Bob Dylan

(e)   Any **three** of: there is no decay in the quality of the recording when a track is copied, such as increased hiss and less detail; effects may easily be changed without having to recopy the master tape; there are many more tracks available – on a multi-track tape, extra tracks could only be freed up through the use of 'bouncing down'; it is cheaper – no need for expensive outboard equipment and reel-to-reel tapes; it is quicker – multi-track editing is a highly skilled, intricate and time-consuming process; the sound is of digital quality, meaning there is a wider and more detailed frequency response; there is a wider range of potential effects available; there is no need for complex lining up and routing of equipment; computer sequencers take up far less space and are more portable: tracks can therefore be recorded or mixed in numerous locations with ease.

Question 8
Jelly Roll Morton and His Orchestra: 'Try Me Out'

(a)   New Orleans jazz

(b)   A left-hand accompaniment style, where it would play a bass note on the first and third beats of the bar and jump up to a chord in a higher register for the second and fourth beats of the bar.

(c)

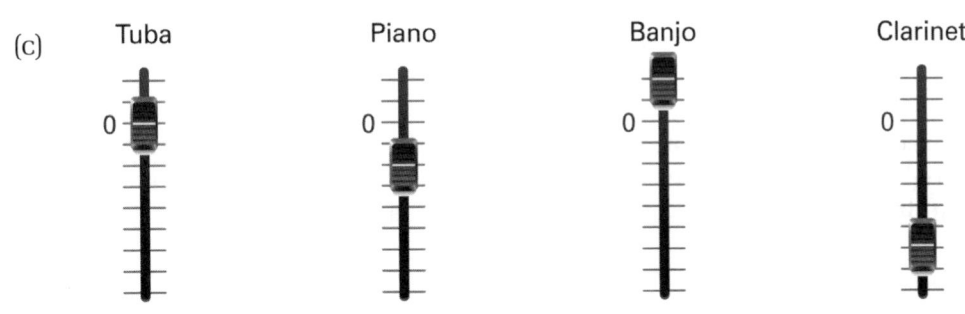

(d)

Shortcoming	How it could be improved
Example: 'wow' producing variations in pitch	**Example:** use time-stretching to cancel out the variations in speed
Unwanted cracks and pops caused by damaged surface of record	Use a click/pop eliminator plug-in
Unwanted hiss and surface noise	Use a filter or EQ to remove the unwanted frequencies; use a noise-reduction plug-in; use Dolby
Narrow frequency range, resulting in poor separation of instruments	Use EQ to boost or reduce frequencies as appropriate to produce a more balanced mix

(e)   78 rpm

Question 9
Rev. James Cleveland: 'Get Right Church'

(a)   Hammond organ

(b)   132 bpm

(c)   (i)

(d)   The soloist and choir interact in a loose call-and-response way (**1**). It is not a strict alternation between the two, however: the soloist's material is an improvisatory, decorative version of the material the choir is singing and falls in and out of time with the choir's entries (**1**).

(e)   Any **three** of: religious theme of text; hand-claps; use of a gospel choir; soulful/improvisatory/ emotional style of singing; typical gospel instrumentation (Hammond organ, piano, tambourine, hand-claps, gospel choir, drum kit, bass).

(f)   The choir sounds too distant (**1**), with a reduced frequency range (**1**), meaning that words are hard to decipher and the rhythmic definition is reduced (**1**). If re-recording the track, the choir should be captured using several regularly spaced condenser mics (**1**) placed a metre or so above and in front of the choir (**1**), to capture a blended but more detailed sound. This can be mixed in with the rest of the instruments as appropriate (**1**).

Question 10
Rihanna: 'Umbrella (Radio Edit)'

(a)   R&B

(b)   Rap/rapping (speaking rhythmically over music)

(c)

(d)   Any **two** of: chorus (on occasional words); delay (with the delayed signal panned to the left and with reverb added); autotune

(e)   Any **four** of: synth strings reduced from several lines to a single line; bass line drops out; piano introduced; snare sample replaced with synthesised hand-clap; bass drum sample replaced with a tighter, shorter one; hi-hat drops out; a second overdubbed vocal is added.

Question 11
Slipknot: 'Wait and Bleed'

(a)   Nu metal

(b)   (iv)

(c)   At 0'00", the vocal line is sung quietly in a low register (**1**). At 0'07" an overdubbed second vocal is introduced, doubling the vocal line for the first part of the phrase (**1**). From 0'12"–0'24", the vocal line is sung more loudly at a higher octave than in previous section (**1**). At 0'28"–0'49" the vocal line is delivered in a guttural half-shouted, half-sung style (**1**). (3 marks total)

(d)   5ths

(e)

Name of parameter	How it changes the signal
Example: make-up gain	Raises or lowers the compressed signal by a specified amount of dB
Attack time	Specifies the length of time allowed to pass before compression is applied
Threshold	Specifies the level of signal that is allowed to pass through the compressor before compression is applied
Compression ratio	Specifies the amount of compression applied: the higher the ratio the more compression is applied
Release time	Specifies the amount of time taken for compression to be removed after the signal drops below the threshold
Gain	Specifies the amount by which the whole signal's level is boosted or attenuated having passed through the compressor
Limiter threshold	Specifies the level at which limiting is applied to the whole signal (to prevent peak distortion)

Question 12
Yes: 'Owner of a Lonely Heart'

(a)   Riff

(b)   (ii)

(c)   It is panned rapidly across the stereo field from hard left to right of centre.

(d)   (i)   Perfect 5th

(ii)   The pitch-shifted signal would need to be time-stretched

(e)   Any **three** of: a new riff is introduced in the bass line; the bass line is doubled by piano; a more regular drum pattern is introduced; a syncopated guitar figure is introduced (panned to the left); a synth strings countermelody is introduced at 2'06"; synth brass are used to highlight the beginning of the section at 1'57", and to highlight the ends of phrases at 2'04" and 2'11".

(f)   Any **two** from: a sampler is an electronic device into which audio samples may be recorded or loaded (**1**) and played back at different speeds (**1**). It enables one or more audio samples to be processed to produce different pitches (**1**), thus turning it into an instrumental timbre that can be triggered by a device such as a controller keyboard or sequencer (**1**).

Section B Questions

13. **Special Focus Style: Rock 'n' Roll (examination years: 2009, 2013)**
    Little Richard: 'Lucille'

(a) Any **three** of: use of blues scale; use of 12 bar-blues chord progression; accented snare on backbeat; use of typical rhythm 'n' blues instrumentation: tenor saxophone, piano, drums, guitar, bass; blues piano style – repeated quavers and triplets in high register; drum fills at ends of phrases; use of turnarounds.

(b) Stop time

(c)

Aspect of recording	Description of problem	Possible solution
Stereo field	**Example:** the recording is in mono	**Example:** re-record the song using multi-track recording techniques, and pan the tracks to form an appropriate stereo image
Gain setting for vocals	There is distortion on the vocals	Re-record the vocal track with the gain at a lower level/with the vocalist further away/with a less sensitive microphone
Clarity of individual instruments	The capture of the individual instruments is poor, resulting in a reduced frequency range and loss of detail	Re-record the song, using standard close-mic techniques, using condenser microphones placed appropriately for each instrument; use EQ
Balance between instruments	Some instruments are masked by others in the mix	Re-record the song using multi-track recording techniques, and adjust the relative levels of the tracks so as to produce a balanced mix

(d) Answers can include (4 marks total): Skiffle was a type of home-made popular music (**1**) that predominated in Britain from 1956–58 (**1**). It was influenced by folk music (**1**), trad jazz (**1**) and rhythm 'n' blues (**1**), and its most notorious exponent was Lonnie Donegan (**1**). It used home-made instruments, such as a tea chest with a broom handle for a bass (**1**) and a washboard as percussion (**1**), and demanded little musical skill (**1**), the guitar part typically involving just three chords. Vocal parts were sung in British accents (**1**). Skiffle was important in enabling young people to be able to form bands with minimal resources (**1**) and fuelled a passion for the popular music coming out of America (**1**), notably folk blues (**1**). Many highly influential British musicians of the 1960s first started in skiffle bands (**1**), including John Lennon and the Quarrymen (**1**) and members of The Who (**1**), before turning to conventional rock 'n' roll instruments. Skiffle thus helped to establish a distinctive British blues-influenced style that became the backbone of British music of the 1960s (**1**).

(e) Answers can include (2 marks for each question):

(i) Bill Haley and The Comets

Bill Haley's hit song *Rock Around the Clock* appeared in the hugely popular film, *Blackboard Jungle* (**1**) (1955). This introduced rock 'n' roll to a wide audience (**1**) through the medium of cinema, and this link was further exploited in the film *Rock Around the Clock* (**1**) (1956), also featuring *Bill Haley and the Comets*. The uninhibited dancing particularly appealed to the teenage audience (**1**), who were enticed by its rebellious nature. *The Comets* also seduced their teenage following with their stage antics (**1**) (with some band members lying on the stage to play their instruments (**1**)), the use of jive-influenced vocals (**1**) (for instance 'Crazy Man Crazy' (**1**)), and took rock 'n' roll outside of America, touring Australia and Europe (**1**).

(ii)   Elvis Presley

The initial appeal of Elvis Presley was his vocal style, which moved effortlessly between country (**1**) and R 'n' B (**1**). Through this, he brought rock 'n' roll to both black and white audiences (**1**), achieving success in the R 'n' B and country charts simultaneously (**1**). His great charisma and sex appeal particularly appealed to women (**1**), while his appearances in films (**1**) such as *Loving You* (**1**), *Jailhouse Rock* (**1**) and *Kid Creole* (**1**) helped to establish him as a household name and further popularise his music. In the late 1950s, a gradual smoothing of his vocal style attracted a broader audience (**1**) and ensured continued commercial success.

(iii)   Cliff Richard

Cliff Richard was largely responsible for creating a distinctively British form of Rock 'n' Roll (**1**), opening up a new British audience for Rock 'n' Roll. Performing with his backing group, The Shadows (**1**), he was marketed as a British equivalent to Elvis Presley (**1**), adopting a similar appearance and performing mannerisms (**1**), and he enjoyed considerable success with 'Move It' (**1**) (1958) and 'Livin' Doll' (**1**) (1959), which were some of the first rock 'n' roll hits produced outside America (**1**). His influence was enhanced by his appearances in films (**1**) such as *The Young Ones* (**1**) (1961) and *Summer Holiday* (**1**) (1963), although by this time his style had moved away from rock 'n' roll, becoming a lighter, 'beat ballad' style (**1**).

14. Special Focus Style: Hip hop (examination years: 2009, 2013)
Missy Elliott: 'Get Ur Freak On'

(a)   Delay (accept echo)

(b)

Timing	Effect
0'28"	(**Example:** b.vox double rap on certain words and phrases to produce chorus effect)
0'30"	(**Example:** shouted exclamation on word 'Ah')
0'35"	High sung note on word 'Nipper'
0'37"–0'40" and 0'45"–0'48"	The word 'yes' is spoken in a lower voice and chorused
0'41"	The syllable 's' is repeated
0'43"–0'44"	A two-note sung phrase is used on the word 'hello', with chorus and reverb

(c)   Retriggering

(d)   Any **four** of: a new, slower-moving, four-note idea is introduced (synthesised violas); this idea is repeated, doubled an octave higher by a synthesised part with heavy use of modulation; a wind noise is introduced; the rap is chorused throughout, with fewer added vocal interjections; the rap repeats a single phrase ('get ur freak on') instead of using continuous prose; the spoken syllable 'gah' is used on the first beat of each bar; the texture, phrase structure and rhythm are more regular and less unpredictable than in the preceding section.

(e)   Answers can include (2 marks total for each question):

(i)   **Toasting:** an early form of rap (**1**) performed by Jamaican DJs (**1**) while they were playing reggae music. It tended to involve short phrases rather than extended rhymes (**1**). Typical themes included boasts about the skill of the DJ (**1**) and general comments about partying (**1**).

(ii)   **Breakdancing:** a style of dancing originally performed in the breakbeat sections (**1**) of early hip hop DJs' sets (**1**). It was very energetic and demanded great strength and agility (**1**), involving headspins, back spins (**1**) and other moves. It frequently involved rival displays of dancing by opposing crews (**1**).

(iii) **Gangsta rap:** covers themes such as sex, violence, drugs, and gang warfare (**1**). It generally has an uncompromising musical style, with strident and percussive samples (**1**) and aggressively delivered lyrics (**1**). Typical examples of gangsta rap include N.W.A., (**1**) Snoop Doggy Dogg (**1**) and Wu-Tang Clan (**1**) (maximum **1** mark for examples of bands).

(iv) **Grime:** a genre of rap that combines hip hop with dance music influences (**1**), notably the breakbeats of UK garage (**1**). It originated in East London in the early 2000s (**1**), with the leading exponent being Dizzee Rascal (**1**), whose albums *Boy in da Corner* (**1**) (2003), *Maths + English* (**1**) (2007) and *Tongue N' Cheek* (**1**) (2009) achieved critical acclaim and mainstream success.

(v) **Breakbeat:** the name for a drum solo (**1**) that often appeared in the middle of funk songs of the 1970s (**1**) (literally a beat played during a 'break' (**1**)). It was characterised by more complex and syncopated drum patterns (**1**) than the drum patterns in the main body of the song. Its complexity conveys a sense of tension and aggression that suits the combative, emotionally charged lyrics of many styles of rap (**1**), creating an undertone of aggression and power.

15. **Special Focus Style: Reggae (examination year: 2010)**
    Jacob Miller: 'Baby I Love You So' and Augustus Pablo: 'King Tubby Meets The Rockers Uptown'

(a) ♩ = 67

(b) Melodica

(c)

	Changes in the Augustus Pablo version
Use of effects	**Example:** extensive use of reverb on the vocals (e.g. 0'09") and both reverb and delay on the melodica (0'17") and guitar (e.g. 0'19").
Use of panning	The panning of the instruments has been changed: vocals now panned to left instead of right of centre, melodica to left of centre instead of right. Or: there is also the use of panning across the stereo field, for instance the melodica up to 0'08", electric guitar at 0'17" and hi-hat at 0'48"
Use of dynamics	The delay on the short instrumental and vocal samples that first appear in 0'16"–0'44" decrease in volume until they fade out (for instance on the vocal phrase 'baby I' from 0'30"–0'33")
Vocal part	Fragments of the original vocal track are used rather than the continuous vocal track of the original, and have effects of reverb and delay
Drum kit part	A faster, more intricate rhythmic pattern is added on a separate hi-hat part

(d) Any **two** of: the use of a remixed version of the tracks of a reggae song, containing changes in panning, balance and the creative omission of certain tracks; application of effects to the original tracks: delay, reverb; creative use of short vocal and instrumental samples taken from the original tracks; creation of space in the mix that would allow a toaster to improvise over the track.

(e) Answers can include (4 marks total for each question):

(i) The Skatalites (formed 1964 (**1**)) were a collective of jazz musicians (**1**) who helped establish and popularise the ska style (**1**) in Jamaica in the 1960s (**1**), forming a bridge between this and reggae (**1**). Their influences, which included swing, bop and blues (**1**), became absorbed into the ska style (**1**), forming a distinctively Jamaican sound. This, together with their instrumentation (trumpet, trombone, saxes, piano, guitar, double bass and drums) (**1**) became central to the reggae style. Well-known singles include 'Addis Ababa' (**1**), 'Guns of Navarone' (**1**), 'Fidel Castro' (**1**) and 'Christine Keeler' (**1**) (maximum **1** mark for examples).

(ii) Bob Marley (1945–81)(**1**) was the most influential reggae artist, securing a global audience (**1**) for the style. In the 1960s his harmony trio, The Wailers (**1**), absorbed the influences of the

Jamaican styles of ska, rude boy and rock steady (**1**) and when, in 1973, he added electric guitars and a female vocalist to the group (**1**), which became known as Bob Marley and the Wailers, his style of reggae gained international popularity. He was also highly influential in making reggae an effective medium for expressing spiritual matters (**1**) and protest (**1**): common themes in his music include Rastafarianism (**1**) and human rights (**1**) in albums like *Survival* (**1**) (1979) and *Uprising* (**1**) (1980) (maximum **1** mark for examples). His impassioned vocal style (**1**) helped in expressing serious subjects like these.

(iii) The Specials (formed 1978 (**1**), becoming Special AKA in 1981 (**1**)) were an English pop group (**1**) who were central to the ska revival (**1**) in Britain in the late seventies and early eighties. They were heavily influenced by 1960s ska (**1**) and also by contemporary British styles of punk and new wave (**1**), bringing a heavier sound to their rhythm section (**1**) and dealing with important social issues of the time (**1**): the fact that they were a multi-racial band during a period of growing racial tension (**1**) was a statement in itself. (Two-tone (**1**)). Like Bob Marley, their music often expressed serious themes, including human rights (**1**) ('Nelson Mandela' (**1**)), the 1981 riots (**1**) ('Ghost Town') (**1**) and rape (**1**) ('The Boiler') (**1**). Their success paved the way for other reggae and ska-influenced British bands (**1**).

16. Special Focus Style: Heavy Rock (examination year 2010)
Van Halen: 'Runnin' with the Devil'

(a) Pitch shifting

(b) The kick drum doubles the bass line throughout. (It is also reinforced by other kit sounds at various other points in the song, e.g. the hi-hat at 3'09"–3'18".)

(c) (i) Trill (**1**), double trill (**1**), use of whammy bar (**1**); (ii) divebomb; (iii) harmonics

(d) Tapping is the use of the fingers of both hands to finger and play notes simultaneously through the use of hammer-ons and pull-offs. It enables a guitarist to play rapid broken chords.

(e) Any **three** of: the consistently high register of the vocal line and the loud volume generate intensity; various falsetto screams and vocalisations ('ooh', 'woo hoo', 'oh yeah', etc.) add to the excitement; spoken motivational phrases, e.g. 'I'll tell you all about it' at 1'17", add to the feeling of 'liveness'; powerful backing vocals on the words 'Runnin' with the devil', sung loudly and in a high register, exude a sense of power.

(f) Any **three** of: by overdriving an amplifier (sending a signal that overloads the amplifier's circuitry); using a 'stomp box'/effects unit; using an amp simulator; feeding the guitar sound into a computer audio sequencer and adding distortion using a plug-in.

(g) **Either**: record the same part twice (**1**) and pan the two tracks to left and right (**1**); **or** by using ADT (**1**) (automatic double tracking (**1**)), which pans two versions of the same track to left and right (**1**), with a short delay between the two (**1**); **or** copy the track and pan the original and the copy to left and right (**1**), with a short delay (**1**) between the two tracks.

(h) Answers can include (2 marks total): Stadium rock is a genre of heavy rock whose music is either suitable for or especially conceived for performance in very large venues (**1**), such as football stadia. Typical features include a fat distorted guitar sound (**1**); virtuoso guitar playing (**1**); powerful drumming (**1**); a heroic style of vocal writing (**1**), often exploiting the high register (**1**); over-the-top stage performances (**1**), perhaps including visual effects such as pyrotechnics (**1**); anthemic choruses (**1**) and a powerful amplified overall sound (**1**).

(i) (i) Answers can include (3 marks total): Led Zeppelin, formed in 1968 (**1**), set the blueprint for many enduring features of heavy rock and heavy metal. The virtuoso playing of lead guitarist Jimmy Page (**1**), who had previously played with The Yardbirds (**1**), set a precedent for the lengthy, complex guitar solos (**1**) of heavy rock and general level of virtuosity (**1**). Their flamboyant performance style (**1**) influenced countless other heavy rock bands: stage performances could last for four hours (**1**) and their audiences grew to immense proportions (**1**), filling football stadia.

This medium of 'stadium rock' (**1**) spawned countless imitators. Their blues-influenced style of guitar playing (**1**) was also influential on many other heavy rock bands. Important albums include *Led Zeppelin (I–IV)* (**1**), *Houses of the Holy* (**1**) and *Physical Graffiti* (**1**) (maximum **1** mark for examples). *Led Zeppelin IV* contains 'Stairway to Heaven' (**1**) and became one of the best-selling albums of all time. Despite their liking for powerful, distorted guitar sounds, they also used instruments not usually associated with heavy rock, such as mandolin (**1**), acoustic guitar (**1**), mellotron (**1**) and synthesisers (**1**).

(ii) Answers can include (3 marks total): Black Sabbath, formed in Birmingham (**1**) in 1968 (**1**), the band concentrated on exploring the darker side of human experience, cultivating a fascination for the themes of horror films (**1**): the occult, death and general destruction (**1**). They devised a musical style to match, often using the 'devil's interval' of the tritone (**1**), employing tuned-down guitar (**1**) to give a darker sound, and using screamed and howled vocal lines (**1**) and very loud, heavily distorted guitars (**1**). This influenced the general sound of most heavy metal subgenres (**1**). The lead singer, Ozzy Osbourne (**1**), was renowned for his on-stage antics (**1**), famously chewing the head off a live bat on stage during a performance (**1**). Notable albums include *Black Sabbath* (**1**), *Paranoid* (**1**), *Master of Reality* (**1**) and *Sabbath, Bloody Sabbath* (**1**) (maximum **1** mark for examples).

(iii) Answers can include (3 marks total): Formed in 1981 (**1**), Metallica are considered to be the main pioneers of the genre of speed metal (**1**). Heavily influenced by Black Sabbath (**1**), Motorhead (**1**) (maximum **1** mark for examples) and British metal bands of the 1980s (**1**), they combined fast tempi (**1**), virtuoso drumming and guitar playing (**1**), tight rhythmic ensemble (**1**) and irregular rhythms (**1**) with the main features of heavy metal generally: dissonant intervals (**1**), heavy guitar distortion (**1**) and extreme loudness (**1**). A common formal device was to contrast highly aggressive sections with quieter brooding ones (**1**), a structure that was subsequently much used in nu-metal and grunge (**1**). The themes of their lyrics tended to focus on raw emotions such as fear and anger (**1**), rather than sexual references (**1**). Notable albums include *Master of the Puppets* (**1**) (1986) and *Metallica* (**1**) (1991) (maximum **1** mark for examples).

17. Special Focus Style: Soul (examination year: 2011)
The Temptations: 'My Girl' and Otis Redding 'My Girl'

(a) Two marks awarded for each feature

Feature	The Temptations	Otis Redding
Texture	Full, busy texture, containing many sustained parts, frequent countermelodies on strings (often in harmony) and antiphony between lead vocal, backing singers, trumpets and saxes; accented backbeat	Cleaner, simplified texture, with fewer countermelodies and less antiphony between instruments; backbeat less accented
Instrumentation	Substantial instrumental forces, including string section, male and female backing singers, trumpets, trombones, alto sax, piano, drum kit, finger clicks, guitar and bass	Smaller instrumental forces: bass guitar, guitars, trumpets, saxes, piano, drum kit (no backing singers or strings)
Separation between instruments	Many of the backing instruments/singers are lost in the mix, which is busy and muddy	All the instruments are clearly heard for the most part throughout
Recording quality	Noticeable distortion, particularly on drums and strings	Cleaner, with no distortion
Ambience	Some reverberation, leading to a warm, blended sound	Drier, resulting in a cleaner, more detailed sound

(b) (i) The 'Wall of Sound' was a technique pioneered by Phil Spector (**1**) and was used extensively on Motown recordings (**1**). It consisted of a rich instrumental arrangement (**1**), typically adding large horn and string sections and backing singers to the standard rock instruments (**1**) (which were themselves often doubled) (**1**), and a rich, blended, reverberant sound quality (**1**).

(2 marks total)

(ii) The effect was created by recording the musicians in a dry studio (**1**), playing the resultant recorded instrumental backing through loudspeakers in a reverberant studio (**1**) and recording this to tape (**1**). Solo vocalists would be recorded in isolation booths (**1**) so that they could be heard in the mix. (2 marks total)

(iii) The instrumentalists could be recorded in a dry studio (**1**) and artificial reverb added (**1**) electronically, through an effects unit (**1**) or using a plug-in (**1**) in sequencing software. (2 marks total)

(c) (i) Answers can include (4 marks total): Booker T & the MGs was the name given to a group of instrumentalists who made up the rhythm section on Stax Records' (**1**) recordings. Comprising a rhythm section (**1**) and usually brass and saxes (**1**), they developed the tight, punchy sound (**1**) that is a feature of 'Southern Soul' (**1**) and which contrasts heavily with the lush Motown arrangements (**1**). They backed artists such as Otis Redding (**1**), Wilson Pickett (**1**) and Sam and Dave (**1**) (maximum **1** mark for examples), performing on tracks such as 'In the Midnight Hour' (**1**) and 'Soul Man' (**1**). They also functioned as a band in their own right, their best known releases including 'Green Onions' (**1**), 'My Sweet Potato' (**1**) and 'Soul Limbo' (**1**) (maximum **1** mark for examples).

(ii) Answers can include (4 marks total): Aretha Franklin was one of the most influential soul singers of the late 1960s (**1**). She was heavily influenced from a young age by gospel music (**1**), singing in her father's Baptist church in Detroit (**1**) and coming into contact with many leading gospel singers, including Mahalia Jackson (**1**), Clara Ward (**1**) and James Cleveland (**1**) (maximum **1** mark for examples). This experience greatly shaped her singing style, which she brought into soul. Signing to Columbia Records (**1**) in 1960 (**1**), she achieved only modest success (**1**), but after signing to Atlantic Records (**1**) in 1966 (**1**) she produced a number of hits (**1**), including 'Respect' (**1**) (1967), 'Chain of Fools' (**1**) (1968), 'Since You've Been Gone' (**1**) (1968), 'Think' (**1**) (1968), 'The House That Jack Built' (**1**) (1968) and 'I Say a Little Prayer' (**1**) (1968) (maximum **1** mark for examples). She wrote her own vocal arrangements for her tracks (**1**), using her gospel experience to create call and response effects (**1**) with her backing singers, *The Sweet Inspirations* (**1**). She sang in many cover versions of other artists (**1**). Her influence waned in the 1970s (**1**) as other Atlantic singers, such as Roberta Flack, came to prominence.

(iii) Answers can include (4 marks total): Marvin Gaye's early influences included gospel (**1**), singing and playing the organ in church (**1**) from a young age, and doo-wop (**1**), singing in the doo-wop group the Marquees (**1**) in the late 1950s on songs for the Chess label (**1**). Motown signed the Marquees in 1961 (**1**) and Gaye had varied roles, appearing as a drummer on Smokey Robinson and the Miracles songs (**1**), and singing in duets with Mary Wells (**1**) ('Once Upon a Time' (**1**)) and Tammi Tyrell (**1**) ('Ain't no Mountain High Enough' (**1**)). His main contribution to soul, however, came when he renegotiated his contract with Motown in 1971 (**1**), gaining artistic control of his records (**1**). He then produced *What's Going On* (**1**), one of soul's first concept albums (**1**), which included protest songs against the Vietnam War (**1**) ('What's Going On' (**1**) and 'Mercy, Mercy Me (The Ecology)' (**1**) (maximum **1** mark for examples)). Later songs became more overtly sexual in nature (**1**), such as 'Let's Get it On' (**1**) and 'Sexual Healing' (**1**) (maximum **1** mark for examples), again taking soul in a new direction. Musically, he incorporated many influences into his music, ranging from gospel (**1**), R&B (**1**), pop (**1**), doo-wop (**1**), funk (**1**), jazz (**1**) and disco (**1**) (maximum **1** mark for examples of style), and his brand of soul was highly influential on other soul artists of the seventies.

18. Special Focus Style: Indie Rock (examination year: 2011)
The Smiths: 'That Joke Isn't Funny Anymore'

(a) Points could include: place a condenser microphone approximately 20cm in front of the fingerboard and away from the sound hole to capture a thinner sound with less body. Choose a microphone with a good high frequency response. Use EQ to roll off lower mid frequencies and boost higher frequencies.

(b) $\frac{6}{8}$

(c) The EQ is boosted in the high frequencies to exaggerate the aspirate, or breathy sound; longer reverb applied.

(d) Analogue mixing desk: turn the pan pot for the track at a constant rate, repeatedly between hard left and hard right.

Computer sequencer: **one** of: use an autopan <u>insert/plug-in</u> (**1**); use an automated pan controller, either drawing the movements on manually or 'recording' them using an external controller or software interface (**1**); move the pan from left to right with a mouse and record those movements (**1**).

(e) Repetition: any **two** of: the lyrics have been repeated; the melody has been repeated; the chord sequence is repeated; the bass line is repeated; the drum pattern is repeated; the countermelody using the high pad sound is repeated.

Variety: any **two** of: a second overdubbed vocal line is introduced (2'38" onwards); the repeated lyric is broken down into shorter phrases and individual words from 2'52" onwards (e.g. 'happening in mine', 'now', 'mine'); small changes are introduced into the bass line, drum pattern, and acoustic (rhythm) guitar part.

(f) Manchester

(g) Any **four** of: dark lyrics on the subject of depression at odds with typically lightweight, image-conscious and materialist subject matter of the time; low-key, understated style of singing contrasts with stylised 'heroic' style favoured by commercial labels; sung in a British rather than American accent; absence of extended guitar solo contrasts with 'guitar hero' style of playing on many eighties rock songs; melodic material is through-composed and doesn't recur throughout the song, so there is not an easy way in for the listener; unusual structure: no obvious verse-chorus structure, so demands more attention from the listener; musically shies away from 'showy' techniques, such as virtuoso drum fills, powerful drumming, etc.; favours a sixties-influenced, jangly acoustic guitar sound rather than the overdriven, electric guitar sound of eighties rock.

(h) (i) Answers can include (4 marks total): The Fall are now recognised as one of the first British indie bands (**1**) and set the blueprint for the Indie band model. Formed in 1977 (**1**) in Manchester (**1**), their guitar-based style was influenced by punk (**1**) but was ultimately unclassifiable (**1**) in terms of conventional genres. Apart from some minor hits in the 1980s, they had limited commercial success (**1**) and owed much of their reputation to the BBC Radio **1** disc jockey John Peel (**1**), who championed their music and invited them to appear on 24 'Peel Sessions' (**1**). The Fall's vocalist, Mark E Smith (**1**), exposited a ranting vocal style (**1**) influenced in part by punk and his biting and oblique lyrics dealt with themes arising from Manchester's popular culture (**1**). The Fall were influential on many indie bands, including Happy Mondays (**1**), Elastica (**1**) and Pavement (**1**) (maximum **1** mark for examples). They have released over 30 albums (**1**), from the hastily recorded *Live at the Witch Trials* (**1**) (1979) to the more commercial, dance-influenced *The Infotainment Scam* (**1**) (1993).

(ii) Answers can include (4 marks total): Factory Records was a Manchester-based (**1**) record label set up in 1978 (**1**) by Tony Wilson (**1**), a British television presenter, initially with Martin Hannett (**1**) as producer, who had produced punk bands such as The Buzzcocks (**1**). Factory Records recruited the bands Joy Division (**1**) (later New Order (**1**)), A Certain Ratio (**1**), The Durutti Column (**1**) and The Happy Mondays (**1**) (maximum **1** mark for examples). They exercised no artistic control over the bands (**1**) on their roster, allowing them to develop their own distinctive styles. In 1981, Factory Records set up the Hacienda nightclub (**1**), which became a venue for local bands to perform and was the focal point for the rave, acid house and techno scene in the late 1980s (**1**). The mixture of music that was heard here was an important influence on groups associated with the Madchester scene (**1**) of 1988, such as Happy Mondays (**1**), James (**1**) and Inspiral Carpets (**1**) (maximum **1** mark for examples), who integrated elements of techno and house into a general post-punk guitar-based indie style (**1**).

(iii) Answers can include (4 marks total): Radiohead, formed in 1988 (**1**), are one of the most successful British indie bands, and are one of the few to have garnered a significant following in America (**1**). Originally a guitar-based band (**1**), their initial releases appealed to a young American middle-class audience, with strong grunge influences (**1**) being evident in their 1992 single, 'Creep' (**1**). The freedom allowed to them by signing to an independent record label meant that they could experiment with more complex structures (**1**), prog rock influences (**1**) and more innovative combinations of timbre (**1**) on their 1997 album *OK Computer* (**1**). The song 'Paranoid Android' (**1**) was especially adventurous, including irregular time signatures (**1**) and through-composed structures (**1**) in the mould of 'Bohemian Rhapsody'. Later albums, such as *Kid A* (**1**) (2000) and *Hail to the Thief* (**1**) (2003) exploit the use of electronics (**1**) and sonic soundscapes (**1**). They were one of the first major bands to take advantage of the internet as a means of distributing their music (**1**): *Kid A* was promoted on the internet without the normal accompaniments of videos, tours or singles, and they later introduced a system of voluntary payments (**1**) for downloading their album *In Rainbows* (**1**) (maximum **1** mark for examples of album names).

19. **Special Focus Style: Punk and New Wave (examination year: 2012)**
    The Clash: 'Career Opportunities'

(a) Major

(b) Timed delay/double delay

(c) Any **four** of: half-sung, half-shouted singing style (1); short song length (1); non-American accent (a British London accent on this track) (1); fast tempo (approximately 184 bpm) (1); lack of extended instrumental solos (1); simple, repeated melodic phrases (1); drum's, bass's and guitar's rhythms are closely tied to the harmonic rhythm (changes of chords) (1); use of distorted electric guitars (1); lyrics dealing with social issues/unemployment (1)

(d)

Problem	Solution
Example: vocalist moving around during performance	**Example:** ask vocalist to stay the same distance away from microphone; set up a pop screen at an appropriate distance from the microphone and ask the vocalist to remain close to the pop screen
Excessive levels due to shouting	Use a dynamic microphone; lower the gain control on the mixing desk
Sudden changes in dynamic levels	Use compression
Unwanted breath and popping noises	Use a pop shield

(e) Any **three** of (2 marks each): because the punk style demanded fairly rudimentary musical skills, this opened it up to more people, whereas progressive rock required considerable musical skill and experience; the anger and aggression that youths needed to express was more suitable for a direct, simple, rhythmic musical style; progressive rock was too complex harmonically and formally to convey these emotions effectively; the lyrics were often crude and repetitive and mostly consisted of short phrases – these suited the short, repetitive melodic phrases of punk rather than the longer, more developed melodic phrases of progressive rock; the shouted style of singing did not blend with the smooth, refined timbres of progressive rock, working better with the rough-and-ready timbres of punk; owing to the small resources that punk demanded, bands could be formed and music created much more easily and cheaply than was the case with progressive rock, which had to be perfected in a studio and required expensive electronic instruments.

(f) (i) Answers can include (4 marks total): The Stooges (1967–1974) were a rock group from the American Midwest (**1**) who are considered to be the 'Godfather of punk' because of their influence on punk bands of the 1970s (**1**). Their lead singer, Iggy Pop (**1**), epitomised the nihilist attitude of some teenagers of the time, with intense, angry performances (**1**) which included rolling around in broken glass on stage (**1**). Their lyrics covered negative and pessimistic themes (**1**) and their musical performances, which were strident and had a home-made quality (**1**), anticipated the 'anyone can make music' attitude (**1**) and feel of punk. Important albums include *Funhouse* (**1**) (1970) and *Raw Power* (**1**) (1973) (maximum **1** mark for examples) and well-known songs include 'Down on the Street' (**1**), 'Loose' (**1**) and 'TV Eye' (**1**) (max **1** mark for examples).

(ii) Answers can include (4 marks total): The Buzzcocks were a Manchester-based band (**1**) formed in 1976 (**1**). Initially a punk band, pop influences led to a gradual softening of their style (**1**) and more commercial success. Features of their early punk style, as displayed in their first album, *Spiral Scratch* (**1**), include repetitive material (**1**), a tight rhythm section (**1**), energetic punk-style guitar playing (**1**) and pop-influenced melodies (**1**). They also subscribed to punk's mission to shock: an early single, 'Orgasm Addict' (**1**) was banned by the BBC (**1**). After several changes of personnel, later songs lost the hard edge of punk, with songs such as 'Ever Fallen in Love (With Someone You Shouldn't've)' (**1**) being influential on new wave bands (**1**). Important albums include *Another Music in a Different Kitchen* (**1**), *Love Bites* (**1**) and *A Different Kind of Tension* (**1**) (maximum **1** mark for examples of albums).

(iii) Answers can include (4 marks total): Gary Numan's Tubeway Army was originally a punk band (**1**), but soon became one of the pioneers of synthpop in Britain (**1**) and one of the leading New Wave bands. Heavily influenced by the sound and robotic performance style of *Kraftwerk* (**1**), their lead singer Gary Numan (**1**) remodelled the sound of the band around synthesisers (**1**), creating futuristic soundscapes (**1**) and devising his own robot-like alter ego (**1**). Gary Numan was important in taking punk's direct musical style and its desire to shock into the realm of synthpop (**1**), creating striking and original songs such as 'Are "Friends" Electric?' (**1**) (1979), 'Cars' (**1**) (1979) and 'We Are Glass' (**1**) (maximum **1** mark for examples), which also proved to be highly successful chart hits. Gary Numan was an important transitional figure between punk and early synthesiser bands (**1**) such as The Human League.

20. Special Focus Style: Club Dance (examination year: 2012)
Sash! and Stunt: 'Raindrops (Encore une fois) [Radio Edit]'

(a) Pitch correction/'Autotune'

(b) A mash-up is a track created by combining two or more existing tracks, commonly the vocal line of one song and the rhythm and accompaniment of another.

(c) Any **two** of: choose the vocal sample required and edit it to the desired length (**1**). Copy and paste it (**1**) with short gaps between the copies (**1**) to fit the required rhythm (**1**). Progressively reduce the volume of the track during this looped section (**1**).

(d) Breakdown

(e) Starting with a single vocal line, more and more tracks are introduced at regular intervals (**1**), creating a powerful sense of expectation (synth riff and synth bass line at 2'06" (**1**); 'feels so lonely' vocal sample at 2'10" (**1**); snare at 2'13" (**1**); 'encore une fois' vocal sample at 2'22" (**1**)); rapid upward frequency sweep/glissando used 2'22"– 2'23" (**1**) to launch into new section; lowpass filter (**1**) with a rising cutoff frequency (**1**) applied to the synth part playing the riff, leading to a progressive brightening of the sound (**1**); there is progressive diminution in the snare drum part (**1**) (crotchets at 2'13", a more intricate rhythm combining semiquavers and quavers at 2'17", repeated semiquavers at 2'20" and repeated demisemiquavers at 2'22" (**1**)).

(f) Any **four** of: extensive use of synthesisers; extensive use of reverb and delay effects on synths and vocal lines to create a spacious feel; off-beat bass line (e.g. 1'08"); typical trance groove of 'four on the floor' kick drum (a hit on each beat of the bar) and snare/hi-hat on the off beat (e.g. 1'01"); fast tempo (120–150 bpm) – this track is 140 bpm; use of breakdown sections, with substantial sections containing no percussion (for instance 0'10" to 0'46").

(g) Any **two** of: trip-hop; big beat; jungle/drum 'n' bass; hardcore; rap/hip hop.

(h) (i) Answers can include (4 marks total): Norman Cook (Fatboy Slim) is credited as being one of the main creators of the 'Big Beat' (**1**) style of dance music that originated in Brighton (**1**) in the late 1990s (**1**). A former guitar player for The Housemartins (**1**), he moved into dance music, achieving success as a remixer (**1**) with songs such as Turn on, Tune in, Cop out (**1**) (1995). DJing as 'Fatboy Slim' at the Big Beat Boutique (**1**) in Brighton, he developed and refined several techniques that became integral to Big Beat, including the use of the TB 303 (**1**) (a Transistor Bass synthesiser (**1**)), creating rhythms by chopping up and recombining vocal samples (**1**), and using progressive diminution in breakdown sections (**1**), particularly in snare and vocal parts (**1**). Well-known remixes include 'Renegade Master' (Wildchild) (**1**), and 'Brimful of Asha' (Cornershop) (**1**) (maximum **1** mark for examples of records).

(ii) Answers can include (4 marks total): Orbital, who came to prominence in the 1990s (**1**) as a techno group (**1**), contributed to the development of dance music by creating a style which combined techno with influences from ambient electronica (**1**). Unlike many other dance acts, they made a point of operating their equipment live in actual performances (**1**) and also of employing visual effects (**1**), adding a new dimension to dance music. The success of their approach was confirmed when they were chosen as a headline act at Glastonbury in 1994 (**1**), a festival which had previously been dominated by rock acts (**1**). Their albums were unusual in dance music for resembling concept albums (**1**), their music being capable of sustaining a long-term musical argument over a large time-scale (**1**) (an example being *Untitled* (**1**)). This versatility led to their being employed in creating film soundtracks (**1**) (such as *Shopping* (**1**) and *Event Horizon* (**1**) (maximum **1** mark for examples), thus helping to establish the use of dance music in new mediums. Orbital tracks differ widely in style, from 'Chime', which is largely ambient electronica (**1**) to 'Satan' (**1**), which is heavily influenced by thrash metal (**1**) and which includes samples of the Butthole Surfers (**1**), securing their reputation for being at the more experimental and eclectic end of dance music.

(iii) Answers can include (4 marks total): The Prodigy were a British band from Essex (**1**) who became one of the leading exponents of hardcore (**1**) in the UK in the 1990s (**1**). They were also one of the first dance acts to achieve the same level of media exposure as conventional pop and rock groups (**1**), due to their UK chart success. They gave frenetic live performances (**1**), leading to numerous tours and festival appearances, helping to establish a new platform for dance music outside of nightclubs (**1**). They developed an idiosyncratic, menacing style (**1**) which combined the breakbeats of hardcore (**1**) with more conventional sounds such as heavy rock guitar, flute, live drums, and punk-tinged vocals, giving them a broader appeal (**1**) than many hardcore acts. They were also important for effecting a transition from hardcore to a more techno-influenced style (**1**), with their original angular melodies (**1**), for instance in 'Everybody in the Place (155 and Rising)' (**1**) giving way to the repetition of simpler ideas (**1**) that is a feature of their 1996 UK no. 1 single, 'Firestarter' (**1**).

A2 Sample Paper 1 Mark Scheme

(80 marks total)

All audio file examples can be found on the *Edexcel A2 Music Technology Listening Tests* CD in the folder 'Mark Schemes/SP1 Sorry MS'.

Question 1 (12 marks)

Question No.	Answer	Mark
1(a)	Listen to candidate file in relation to 'TK1 Sorry EXAMPLE EP.wav'. Is an electric piano assigned? Suitable electric piano (EP), Rhodes, Wurlitzer etc. (2) An EP-sounding synthesiser (1) Guitar, normal piano or any other sound: no marks (0)	2

Question No.	Answer	Mark
1(b)	Listen to candidate file in relation to 'TK1 Sorry EXAMPLE EP.wav'. The right-hand notes between bars 11 and 14 must not sustain or blur. There are seven pedal on/off events; one during each chord of the EP All sustain controls removed (2) Two or more sustain controls removed but not all (1) One control event removed or the wrong events changed (0)	2

Question No.	Answer	Mark
1(c)	Pan (1)	1

Question No.	Answer				Mark
		Data 1	**Data 2**	**Range of values**	
1(d)	Controller	01 (1) or Modulation wheel (1)	64 (1) or 63 (1)	1–128 (1) or 0–127 (1)	3

Question No.	Answer	Mark
1(e)	Listen to candidate file in relation to 'TK1 Sorry EXAMPLE EP.wav' (i) Bar 9 F♯ deleted (1); if anything else is deleted or the F♯ deleted (0) (ii) Bar 12 'B' one semitone lower (1); if the B has not been changed or a different note changed (0) (iii) Bar 17 four notes all should be lengthened (1); if no notes are lengthened or the wrong notes changed (0) (iv) Bar 28 add end note (1); if note added is correct but at low velocity (½); if no note is added or the wrong note added (0) All changes should sound as in example file 'TK1 Sorry EXAMPLE EP.wav'	4

Question 2 (18 marks)

Question No.	Answer	Mark
2(a)	Listen to candidate file in relation to 'TK2 Sorry EXAMPLE drums.wav'. The order of the drums should match the file above. NOTE for quicker marking: Bar 12 and onwards: clap instead of snare Bars 1 and 11: fills Bars 19–20: different fill Bar 21: cymbals start Bar 22–23: listen for tambourine continuity Bar 23 to end: slowing down section – this will not fit anywhere but the end Other errors could be: Music not placed exactly in time with metronome, glitches/audible joins/gaps/digital clicks between the parts	
	Excellent accuracy of editing	6
	A few small slips which do not detract from the overall performance	5
	Several errors	3–4
	Some significant intrusive errors and/or omissions, with unmusical effect	2
	Limited accuracy, seriously compromising the performance	1
	Not present as a separately recorded track	0

Question No.	Answer	Mark
2(b)	A brief definition should be provided along with each parameter's relationship to the other parameters (if appropriate) to gain full marks. (i) Compressor: a tool that can reduce or limit (1) the dynamic range (1) of audio material (ii) Threshold: the input volume (dynamic level, amplitude) at which the compressor starts working (1). Material/audio with a dynamic range above or over the threshold will be compressed/operated on (1) (iii) Ratio: the amount the audio material above the threshold is dynamically reduced (1). A ratio of 2:1 for example: when input audio material is 2dB over the threshold the output level will be reduced to only 1dB above (1) (iv) Attack: the time/speed the compressor will take to respond (reach the full ratio dynamic range reduction) to audio material (1) above the threshold (1) (v) Release: the time/speed at which the compressor will hold on to audio material (1) after it is below the threshold (1) (vi) Gain: makes up for the loss of level (1) after the compressor. Often known as make-up gain (1)	12

Question 3 (16 marks)

Question No.	Answer	Mark
3(a)	For melodic errors see scores below. Two marks available for each correct answer up to a maximum of 4 marks; 1 mark for identifying the error and 1 mark for rewriting the complete corrected bar. Bar 14 first quaver should be an E♭ not a B♭ (2) Bar 17 first quaver should be an E♭ not a C (2) Bar 19 fourth quaver should be a C not a G (2) 	4

Question No.	Answer	Mark
3(b)	For rhythmic errors see scores below. Two marks available for each correct answer up to a maximum of 4 marks; 1 mark for identifying the error and 1 mark for rewriting the complete corrected bar. Bar 15 beat 4 should be a quaver rest followed by a quaver (2) Bar 21 beat 3 should be two quavers (rather than a dotted quaver followed by semiquaver) (2) 	4

Question No.	Answer	Mark
3(c)	Overdubbing (2); any other answers (0)	2

Question No.	Answer	Mark
3(d)		6

(i) A drawing with a true likeness to the pattern above (2). A pattern that indicates the sides are larger than the front pick-up, but still retains the correct overall shape (1). A drawing that indicates the 'D' lobe but adds a 'X' lobe or changes the D shape so that it is not similar to the above (0)

(ii) A cardioid polar pattern is directional in pick-up and most sensitive to sound arriving head on (on-axis) to the flat face of the diaphragm and to a lesser extent the sides of the diaphragm. If a D is placed in either of the positions in the picture above (1)

(iii) A cardioid polar pattern is not sensitive to sound from behind; the X should only be placed in the indent of the cardioid pattern (1)

(iv) Any one of the following: omnidirectional, figure of eight or bi-directional, shotgun, supercardioid, hypercardioid (2)

Note: If no pattern is drawn, no marks can be awarded for Qu3 (d) i, ii or iii

Question 4 (16 marks)

The answers given below are intended as a guide. Alternative answers will always receive credit if they form an accurate and unambiguous response to the question posed. The mark total awarded for this question is 16. Please note, more than 16 possible marks are listed here.

Analogue tape comprises three main properties: a thin and long plastic strip (cellulose acetate (1)) that is wound onto a spool or reel (1), with a magnetic coating (1) (iron oxide (1)) attached with a binder (1). The binder glues or attaches the magnetic coating to the plastic strip (1).

Analogue tape is able to store a magnetic representation of changes in an electronic circuit (1) on its magnetic coating via a tape recorder (1). A typical tape recorder/player comprises the following elements in order that the supply-reel tape is pulled though the device by the capstan to the take-up reel tape:

Supply reel (1) – storage depositary for tape that is ready to be recorded or played (1)

Tension arm (1) – keeps the supply-reel tape taut (1)

Idle roller (1) – positions the tape at the correct angle for the guide (1)

Guide (1) – lines the tape up for the erase head (1)

Erase head (1) – clears any previous magnetic changes (1)

Tape lifters (1) – raise the tape away from the tape heads (1) (to prevent wear (1)) only during fast forward or rewind (1)

Record head (1) – realigns the magnetic data on the tape to match the analogue (electronic voltage change) signal that it receives (1) or writes the analogue material to the tape (1)

Play head (1) – reads the magnetic changes on the tape and converts them back to tape recorder circuitry as changes in electronic voltage (1)

Capstan (1) – controls the speed of the tape (1) past the tape record and play heads (1)

Pinch roller (1) – forces the tape against the capstan to achieve even grip by the capstan and therefore even speed of the tape (1)

Second tension arm (1) – keeps the tape on the take-up reel taut (no extra marks if mentioned above on supply reel)

Take-up reel (1) – depositary for recorded tape (1).

Speed of tape in relation to quality: the speed of a tape record/player is controlled by the capstan, which turns at a constant speed (set by the user or manufacturer) (1). The speed of a tape recorder is often set and measured in IPS (inches per second) (1). A typical open reel (reel-to-reel) tape machine runs at 30 IPS, 15 IPS, 7½ IPS or 3¾ IPS; while a compact cassette tape runs at a comparatively slow 1⅞ IPS (1) (award 1 mark only for a typical tape speed). The faster a tape speed the higher the quality of high frequency presence in a recording and the lower the background noise or hiss (1). Other factors such as tape width (1), tape chemical properties (not all tape is the same), binder formulation and thickness also affect the quality of a recording (1).

Track count (1): the number of tracks that can be recorded or overdubbed onto tape depends on the width of the tape (1) and the number of record heads on the tape recorder (1). The following represent standard tape widths and track counts achievable: 2-inch tape 16–24 tracks (1), 1-inch tape 4–16 tracks (1), ½-inch tape 2–16 tracks (1), ¼-inch tape 1–8 tracks (1) and ⅛-inch tape 2–8 tracks (1). A tape machine with two heads is capable of recording two tracks independently (1), while one with 24 heads is capable of recording 24 tracks independently (1). As a general rule, the wider a tape, the more tracks it is capable of recording independently (1).

Wow and flutter (1): if the capstan turns unevenly on its axis or if the motor varies in speed (1), 'wow and flutter' will be introduced to the recording. The effect of wow and flutter is a change in pitch from the normal for all recorded data/music on that part of the tape (1). A poor tape recorder may introduce wow and flutter during the recording process and these pitch changes would play back every time with the same pitch variation (even on a tape machine with perfect motor/capstan stability) as wow and flutter (1). Of course a perfect recording may suffer from wow and flutter if played back through a poor quality machine (1).

Linear tracking format, cutting and splicing (1): analogue tape is a linear tracking format (1). To get to the chorus of a track recorded verse and chorus etc. you would first have to physically play or fast-forward through the verse (1) (unlike digital recording). Editing a performance on tape is possible by physically cutting and splicing two different parts of a tape or different tapes (1).

Tape saturation (1): the overload of a magnetic tape due to an input signal that is too high/loud passing from the record head to the tape (1). Mild tape saturation often results in a warm rich sound and is associated with some of the best qualities of tape recording (1). A tape's saturation point is reached when an increase in the input signal or magnetising force cannot produce an equivalent increase in magnetisation of the tape's magnetic coating (1).

Tape maintenance (1): tape heads require cleaning to remove oxide build up (1) (actual particles from the tape).

Frequency response (1): unlike digital, the analogue tape recording process almost always introduces sound frequencies into a recording in a non-linear frequency (not flat) manner in relation to the input signal frequency (1). Non-linear frequency response can be corrected in part by adjusting a tape machine's AC bias and matching this to the specific type or formula of tape used (1), also through using EQ (1).

Noise reduction (1): to combat tape hiss (1) and other unwanted tape noise, noise reduction (NR) encoding/decoding systems were developed by companies such as Dolby (1) and dbx (1). Dolby Type A NR, for example, increases the amplitude in four bands during recording to tape/encoding (1, accept 'boosts HF') and decreases them proportionally during decoding/tape playback (1). NR alters frequency response of the audio material, although not always in the audible frequency (1).

As storage format, tape will degrade over time, especially if not kept in an optimum environment, so archivists periodically backup all old tapes to new ones (1). Every time an analogue tape is copied, quality decreases (1).

Question 5 (18 marks)

Listen to file 'TK3 Sorry EXAMPLE mix.wav' before marking answers.

(a)   (3 marks)

Marks	Management and controlling dynamics, vocal track
3	Excellent control so that the vocal sits in the mix and the detail in the quieter sections is brought out; no pumping or squashed sound. The vocal is even and smooth
2	Competently handled but the vocal occasionally sounds squashed, pumps or jumps out too much
1	Poorly handled so that vocal sounds squashed, pumps or jumps out, and does not sit well in the mix
0	No compression can be identified on the vocal No mix present on CD

(b) (3 marks)

Marks	Management and controlling EQ of bass track
3	Excellent control so that bass sits in the mix without extreme frequency exaggeration or restriction (NOTE: A low frequency boost EQ from approximately 200Hz down should have been added to compensate for weak bass)
2	Competently handled with some misjudgements, bass occasionally booms
1	EQ applied poorly, with extreme settings. Bass booms, or top/mid are over emphasised
0	No EQ can be identified No mix present on CD

(c) (3 marks)

Marks	Management and control of stereo delay on the electric piano (EP)
3	Excellent use of stereo delay effect enhances the end of the EP line. Delay is not too fast or slow and auto pans to a short tail (NOTE: a stereo tap delay should have been added that does not have too much feedback)
2	Competent stereo delay effect, but repetitions are slightly too fast or slow and/or carry on for just a little too long or not at all (NOTE: two taps min)
1	Poorly managed stereo delay effect – in mono, or distorts due to too much feedback, is too long or too short so as to sound silly
0	No stereo delay can be heard on the EP at the end or it is added elsewhere in the track No mix present on CD

(d) (3 marks)

Marks	Application of reverb
3	Excellent use of reverb on all tracks. (NOTE: a 1.5 second reverb max. would be appropriate for this track)
2	Competent use of reverb with some misjudgements
1	Serious misjudgement on one track or more. Vocal is swamped or has been added to the bass in significant amounts
0	No use of reverb on any track No mix present on CD

(e) (3 marks)

Marks	Balance and blend
3	Consistently well balanced and effectively blended across all parts of the mix. (NOTE: each track should be clearly heard. However, the vocal should be slightly forward in the mix)
2	Most tracks are well balanced. A minor slip in one part
1	Poorly balanced, detrimental to the musical outcome. Vocal back in mix or one instrument too loud consistently
0	Not all tracks present No mix on CD

(f)   (3 marks)

Marks	Presentation of mix
3	Beginning and end of mix does not cut out music, reverb tail or stereo multi-tap delay. The beginning should have 0.2–1 seconds of silence before the music starts. The mix output should be near normalised with no distortion
2	Beginning and end of mix does not cut out music or reverb tail. The beginning has a silence of greater than 1 second. The mix output should be near normalised with no distortion
1	Beginning and end of mix does not cut out music. Reverb tail may be cut out. The beginning has a silence of greater than 1 second. The mix output is too low or too high or in places distorts
0	Parts of the song are missing, for example the start or end are cut off. The mix output is too low or too high or consistently distorts
	No mix present on CD

A2 Sample Paper 2 Mark Scheme

(80 marks total)

All audio file examples can be found on the *Edexcel A2 Music Technology Listening Tests* CD in the folder 'Mark Schemes/SP2 Holler MS'.

Question 1 (14 marks)

Question No.	Answer	Mark
1(a)	Melodic errors: see scores below. 2 marks for each correct answer up to a maximum 4 marks total; 1 mark for identifying the error and 1 mark for writing down the correct note on the stave.	4
	For melodic errors see scores below. Two marks available for each correct answer up to a maximum of 4 marks; 1 mark for identifying the error and 1 mark for rewriting the complete corrected bar.	
	Bar 6 – second quaver should be an E top space of the treble clef stave (one octave higher) (2)	
	Bar 14 – last semiquaver should be an E not an A (2)	
	Bar 21 – first dotted-quaver should be an A not a D (2)	

Question No.	Answer	Mark
1(b)	Rhythmic errors: see scores below. 2 marks for each correct answer up to a maximum 4 marks total; 1 mark for identifying/circling the error and 1 mark for writing down the correct note length(s) above the stave. For rhythmic errors see scores below. Two marks available for each correct answer up to a maximum of 4 marks; 1 mark for identifying the error and 1 mark for rewriting the complete corrected bar. Bar 7 – beat 1 should be a crotchet, not a semibreve. (2) Bar 12 – beat 1 should be two quavers, not a semiquaver followed by a dotted quaver. (2) Sea - sons, we tend_____ and_____ sa -	4

Question No.	Answer	Mark
1(c)	To gain full marks, the candidate must reference each control, where appropriate, to the other.	6
(i)	**Frequency:** measured in Hz (1), the point at which audio material will be altered by the EQ gain (boost or cut) (1)	
(ii)	**Q:** The size or width of the frequency range around the frequency point that audio material will be altered. (1) A high 'Q' value results in a small frequency range either side of the frequency point being made available to the gain control. (1)	
(iii)	**Gain:** the amount of boost or cut (1) applied to the audio material at a frequency point (1)	

Question 2 (18 marks)

Question No.	Answer	Mark
2(a)	Listen to candidate file in relation to 'TK1 Holler EXAMPLE bass.wav' (bars 1–7).	
	Excellent – a relatively quick fade that finishes before the change of harmony in the piano	3
	Good – fade works, yet slightly overlaps the new harmony to create dissonance or is slightly too short	2
	Poor – fade is too long or too fast (short) abrupt, not even, clicks or cuts out	1
	No fade, in unaltered state or not present as part of the separately recorded track	0

Question No.	Answer	Mark
2(b)	Listen to candidate file in relation to 'TK1 Holler EXAMPLE bass.wav' bars–end	
	Excellent – correct bass file restarts at bar 13 and is cut from bar 23 just before beat 3 or does not sound after the cross fade into the later file (see later)	3
	Good – starts at the correct location but sounds on so that the glitch in bar 23 beat 3 is heard	2
	Poor – starts in the correct location but sounds on after Holler 04 bass.wav	1
	Starts at the wrong bar, in unaltered state or not present as part of the separately record track	0

Question No.	Answer	Mark
2(c)	Listen to candidate file in relation to 'TK1 Holler EXAMPLE bass.wav' bars 22–24	
	Excellent – volume of the new bass line matches the original seamlessly	4
	Good – volume is very similar to the previous file, but is slightly louder or softer	3
	Poor – volume is too loud or soft and stands out slightly awkwardly	2
	Extremely poor – very little attempt has been made to modify the original or the volume is at the extremes of dynamic range, and inappropriate or distorts	1
	The file is unaltered or not present as part of the separately recorded track	0

Question No.	Answer	Mark
2(d)	Listen to candidate file in relation to 'TK1 Holler EXAMPLE bass.wav' bars 22–24	
	Excellent – no errors evident, seamless cross-fade	4
	Good – but there is a slight error: timing is slightly out in either direction or there is a slight glitch (not noticeable when listened with other tracks)	3
	Poor – noticeable timing error (location) and/or a click is heard or a volume drop during the fade	2
	Extremely poor – the file is a long way off the correct location, pops noticeably or has large volume discrepancies	1
	The file is as original Holler 03 bass.wav (has two audible glitches and does not fade) or not present as part of the separately recorded track	0

Question No.	Answer	Mark
2(e) (i)	**Microphone:** Low-impedance input (1) with a high sensitivity (1) and generally a large amount of gain (1). The approximate sensitivity range of a microphone input is between -80 dBu to -20 dBu (1)	2
(ii)	**Line:** Higher-impedance input than a microphone (1), with lower sensitivity (1) and lower amount of gain or sometimes attenuation for very hot signals (1). Professional line level signal is rated at a nominal level of +4 dBu (1)	2

Question 3 (14 marks)

Question No.	Answer	Mark
3(a)	Listen to candidate file in relation to 'TK2 Holler EXAMPLE drums.wav', bars 2–5	
	Excellent – file is in the correct location	1
	File is not in the correct location or not present as a part of a separately recorded track	0

Question No.	Answer	Mark
3(b)	Listen to candidate file in relation to 'TK2 Holler EXAMPLE drums.wav', bars 13–14	
	Excellent – file is in the correct location	1
	File is not in the correct location or not present as a part of a separately recorded track	0

Question No.	Answer	Mark
3(c)	Listen to candidate file in relation to 'TK2 Holler EXAMPLE drums.wav', bars 15–18	
	Excellent – file is in the correct start location and loops seamlessly	3
	Good – the file is in the correct location but does not loop fully	2
	Poor – the file is in the correct location but does not loop at all	1
	File is not in the correct location or not present as a part of a separately recorded track	0

Question No.	Answer	Mark
3(d)	Listen to candidate file in relation to 'TK2 Holler EXAMPLE drums.wav', bar 19	
	Excellent – file is in the correct location and both the guiro sounds are removed	3
	Good – the file is in the correct location but overlaps new files with a slight glitch	2
	Poor – the file is in the correct location but neither guiro sound is removed, or a considerable glitch is heard	1
	File is not in the correct location or not present as a part of a separately recorded track	0

Question No.	Answer	Mark
3(e)	Listen to candidate file in relation to 'TK2 Holler EXAMPLE drums.wav', bars 20–25	
	Excellent – file is in the correct location	1
	File is not in the correct location or not present as a part of a separately recorded track	0

Question No.	Answer	Mark
3(f)	54	1

Question No.	Answer	Mark
3(g)	Kick 2 (1); the bass drum (1); the two notes of the bass drum that start at 2.1.1.16 and 2.1.2.232 (1).	1

Question No.	Answer	Mark
3(h)	100	1

Question No.	Answer	Mark
3(i)	Programming mistake: pan controller 10 is set fully right or 127 (1); the drums will only sound out of the right-hand speaker (1). Correction: data 2, for pan controller 10, should be changed to 64 (accept 63) or the centre position (1).	2

Question 4 (16 marks)

The answers given below are intended as a guide. Alternative answers will always receive credit if they form an accurate and unambiguous response to the question posed. The mark total awarded for this question is 16. Please note, more than 16 possible marks are listed here.

Unlike most other musical instruments an analogue synthesiser's sound is produced by entirely electronic means (1). Analogue synthesiser operation can be divided into three main areas:

1.   An electronic sound source (1).

2.   Electronic control modules that shape/vary the sound source's output (1).

3.   A trigger that activates a sound source (1).

Analogue synthesisers come in many form factors but the two most common are: modular/semi-modular systems (1) or integrated all-in-one systems (1) such as the Roland SH-09 (1). Both integrated and modular synthesisers use the same electronic signal processing technology, but modular synthesisers are expandable – more modules can be added (1). Modular synthesisers are made up from lots of different electronic units (modules) that have inputs and outputs for each section (1). The modules are joined by patch leads (1). The output signal of one module is fed into the input of another module thus altering the electronic signal (1). Even the keyboard or means of triggering the synthesiser on most modular systems requires patching to the sound source (1). An integrated synthesiser is not expandable and most often does not require patch cables to route the electronic signals to the different internal modules (1); the manufacturer either decides which internal modules follow in a logical manner from the source, or includes switch(es) for the user to change the routing (1).

Sound source: a VCO or voltage controlled oscillator (1) is the most common type of sound source for an analogue synthesiser. A VCO generates a change in voltage that is output via an electric circuit as frequency/pitch (1). If an analogue synthesiser has only one VCO source it will only produce one pitched note at a time (1) (monophonic (1)). If one or more VCOs are employed the synthesiser will be capable of more than one note (1) (polyphonic (1)).

In much the same way two different instruments, a violin and a piano for example, can both produce 'A' at 440 Hz but sound different; so too can a VCO output different types of source wave (1) as follows: sine wave (1), sawtooth wave (1), square wave (1) often with variable pulse width (1), and triangle wave (1).

Another form of sound source is a noise generator (1). White noise and pink noise are good examples for this (1). A white noise generator produces random signals (1). A white or pink noise generator is almost always a secondary module or sound source to a synthesiser's VCO section. It is often combined with a VCO to create more complex sounds like drums or cymbals (1).

Sound shaping: to add interest to the pure sound of the VCO section, the output of a VCO is almost always fed into another module or section such as a VCF. A VCF (1) or voltage controlled filter (1) allows the user to cut or attenuate certain frequencies of the input signal (1). A VCF generally features cutoff (1) and resonance (1) controllers. A cutoff slider or pot (potentiometer) sets the frequency above or below which attenuation starts in a filter (1). A resonance pot adjusts the characteristic of a filter that boosts frequencies around the cutoff frequency (1). Usually a low-pass filter (1), but sometimes a band-pass filter (1) or high-pass filter (1).

Another controller is a VCA (1) or voltage controlled amplifier (1), which allows the user to boost or cut the volume/amplitude of the incoming signal.

An LFO (1) or low frequency oscillator (1), while strictly a signal generator (like a VCO), is often used to control the output voltage of another VCO and not used on its own (1). LFOs can modulate a filter or oscillator in synchronisation with its low frequency output (1). An LFO outputs low frequencies generally below 30 Hz maximum. An LFO applied to a VCO will generate a vibrato effect (1), while applied to a VCA will produce a tremolo effect (1).

Both VCFs and VCAs can affect the sound of the VCO but cannot control this over time without the aid of an envelope (1). An envelope generator (EG) (1) is a circuit that outputs a control signal that can affect the input signal over time (1). The most common type of EG is an ADSR (1) generator. ADSR stands for attack (1) decay (1) sustain (1) and release (1) (maximum 2 marks). The attack is the time the input sound takes to reach its initial peak (1). The decay phase of an envelope starts the moment the attack has attained its peak and is the roll off sound from the peak (1). The sustain level is maintained until the performer lets go of the keyboard trigger (1). The moment the trigger is released the envelope goes into the release phase (1), which is the time taken for the sound to fade away (1). An ADSR most often controls the output of a VCF or VCA (1). However, it can be routed in a modular synthesiser to control other modules too (1).

Triggering or playing a synthesiser: in order for an analogue synthesiser to be played as a musical instrument it must be triggered (1). The trigger requires a control voltage (1) or CV (1) to tell the oscillator what pitch to produce (1) or filter frequency (1) and a gate (1) to open or close the electric circuit (1). The most common type of trigger is a keyboard (1); in an analogue synthesiser a keyboard most often functions as both a CV and a gate (1). A CV sets the pitch of the oscillator (VCO) (1) while a gate turns the CV on (note depressed) or off (note released) (1).

Many analogue synthesisers also feature a mixer section (1). A mixer section allows the users to balance the level between the different oscillators and sub-oscillators (1) (other VCOs or LFOs for example) to arrive at the sound they want.

Analogue synthesisers often feature other controls to allow the user to adjust the pitch of the VCO or cutoff an envelope without retriggering the note (1). A pitch bend controller (1) can be used to adjust the frequency/voltage of the VCO in relation to the note triggered (1). On most analogue synthesisers, pitch bend can also be assigned to control non-pitch function too (1). Another control function is portamento. Portamento is an effect that allows the user to glide between two notes at a gradual rate (1). Portamento varies the voltage incrementally between the two notes (1) at a speed set by the user (1).

Question 5 (18 marks)

Listen to file 'TK3 Holler EXAMPLE mix.wav' before marking answers.

(5a) (3 marks)

Marks	Management and controlling EQ of piano
3	Excellent control so that piano sits in the mix without extreme frequency exaggeration or restriction. (NOTE: A high frequency boost EQ from approximately 500 Hz up should have been added to compensate for the dull piano.)
2	Competently handled with some misjudgements, piano occasionally lacks for presence or booms
1	EQ applied poorly, with extreme settings. Lows, mids or highs boom or are too shrill, or are over emphasised
0	No EQ can be identified, or as the original file
	No mix present on CD

(5b) (3 marks)

Marks	Management and controlling dynamics, vocal
3	Excellent control so that the vocal sits in the mix and the detail in the quieter sections is brought out; no pumping or squashed sound. The vocal is even and smooth
2	Competently handled but the vocal occasionally sounds squashed, pumps or jumps out too much
1	Poorly handled so that vocal sounds squashed, pumps or jumps out, and does not sit well in the mix
0	No compression can be identified on the vocal
	No mix present on CD

(5c) (3 marks)

Marks	Management and control of stereo delay on the drums/snare hits
3	Excellent use of stereo pan effect enhances the second entrance of the drums/snare. Left/right pan should not be extreme
2	Competent stereo pan but it is too extreme or subtle
1	Poorly managed pan that moves halfway through the hit, is not clean or fails to return to centre pan from bar 14
0	No stereo pan can be heard on the snare or it is added elsewhere in the track.
	No mix present on CD

(5d) (3 marks)

Marks	Application of reverb
3	Excellent use of reverb on **all** tracks. (NOTE: It is unlikely that a reverb time of over 1 second would be appropriate for this track.)
2	Competent use of reverb with some misjudgements
1	Serious misjudgement on one or more tracks. Vocal is swamped or reverb has been added to the bass in significant amounts to wash out the track or make it sound too distant, for example
0	No use of reverb on any track No mix present on CD

(5e) (3 marks)

Marks	Balance and blend
3	Consistently well balanced and effectively blended across all parts of the mix. (NOTE: Each track should be clearly heard. However, the vocal should be slightly forward in the mix.)
2	Most tracks are well balanced. A minor slip in one part
1	Poorly balanced, detrimental to the musical outcome. Vocal back in mix or one instrument too loud
0	Not all tracks present No mix on CD

(5f) (3 marks)

Marks	Presentation of mix
3	Beginning and end of mix do not cut out music/reverb tail. The beginning should have 0.2–1 seconds of silence before the music starts. The mix output should be near normalised with no distortion
2	Beginning and end of mix does not cut out music reverb tail or piano sustain. The beginning has a silence of greater than 1 second. The mix output should be near normalised with no distortion
1	Beginning and end of mix does not cut out music. Reverb tail or piano sustain may be slightly cut off. The beginning has a silence of greater than 1 second. The mix output is too low or too high or distorts in places
0	Parts of the song are missing, e.g. cut off at the start/end. The mix output is too low or too high or consistently distorts No mix present on CD

Sample Paper 3 Mark Scheme

(80 marks total)

All audio file examples can be found on the *Edexcel A2 Music Technology Listening Tests* CD in the folder 'Mark Schemes/SP3 Mercutio MS'.

Question 1 (19 marks)

Question No.	Answer	Mark
1(a)	Listen to candidate file in relation to 'TK1 Merc EXAMPLE Vocal.wav' bar 21	
	Excellent – new gain on correct section matches the previous vocal volume	4
	Good – new gain is marginally too high or low in relation to the surrounding vocal audio	3
	Inconsistent – new gain is too high or low in relation to the surrounding audio and/or part of the surrounding audio has been gained up/down. But this is still an improvement on the original.	2
	Poor – new gain is not much better than the original and/or other errors have been introduced	1
	File not present or in unaltered state	0

Question No.	Answer	Mark
1(b)	Listen to candidate file in relation to 'TK1 Merc EXAMPLE Vocal.wav' bars 23–end	
	Excellent – the pitch of the vocals from bar 23 inclusive to the end has been raised by one semitone with no glitching	4
	Good – the pitch has been corrected but the wrong algorithm has been used so the new file slightly glitches or contains up to two artefacts	3
	Fair attempt – the pitch is a little off from true or new pitch contains three or more artefacts	2
	Poor – the pitch is going in the correct direction better than original but still off or pitch is correct but too many noises have been introduced to be usable	1
	File not present, or in unaltered state, or lower in pitch with much glitching	0

Question No.	Answer	Mark
1(c)	The proximity effect is an increase in bass frequency response (1) in a non-linear fashion when a sound source (bass singer or low instrument in particular – optional) is close (1) to a directional microphone. (1)	3

Question No.	Answer	Mark
1(d)	For melodic errors see scores below. Two marks available for each correct answer up to a maximum of 4 marks; 1 mark for identifying the error and 1 mark for rewriting the complete corrected bar. Bar 12 – last crotchet should be B♭ not a C (2) *12* Bars 14 – first semiquaver should be a C not a D (2) *14* Bar 20 – sixth quaver of bar should be an B not an E (2) *20* 	4

Question No.	Answer	Mark
1(e)	Rhythmic errors: see scores below. 2 marks for each correct answer up to a maximum 4 marks total, 1 mark for identifying/circling the error and 1 mark for rewriting the complete corrected bar. Bar 10 – beat 1 should be a staccato crotchet, not a minim (also give full marks for a quaver with no staccato). (2) *10* Bar 18 – beat 1 should be two quavers, not a dotted quaver followed by a semiquaver. (2) *18* 	4

Question 2 (18 marks)

Question No.	Answer	Mark
2(a)	Listen to candidate file 'TK2 Merc EXAMPLE guitar.wav' bar 16	
	Excellent – accidental string noise is removed with no other audio removed	4
	Good – the string noise is removed but a tiny amount of 'good' audio from before or after has also been removed	3
	Poor – noise has been partly removed or fully removed but a noticeable amount of other 'good' audio material has been moved too	2
	Extremely poor – noise is still present and or much of the surrounding guitar line has been disturbed	1
	The file is unaltered or worse or not present as part of the separately recorded track	0

Question No.	Answer	Mark
2(b)	Listen to candidate file 'TK2 Merc EXAMPLE guitar.wav' bars 1–7	
	Excellent – no errors evident (timing spot on)	4
	Good – but there is a slight error: file is a few milliseconds out or a slight glitch exists	3
	Poor – noticeable timing error (location) and or a click is heard	2
	Extremely poor – the file is a long way off the correct location or pops noticeably	1
	The file is unaltered or worse (speaking is still present) or not present as part of the separately recorded track	0

Question No.	Answer	Mark
2(c)	Listen to candidate file 'TK2 Merc EXAMPLE guitar.wav' bars 21–26	
	Excellent – no errors evident. A seamless cross-fade file in correct position	4
	Good – but there is a slight error: file is a millisecond or two out in either direction or is a slight glitch (not noticeable when listened with other tracks)	3
	Poor – noticeable timing error (location) and or a click is heard	2
	Extremely poor – the file is a long way off the correct location or pops noticeably	1
	The file is unaltered or worse (speaking is still present) or not present as part of the separately recorded track	0

Question No.	Answer	Mark
2(d)	DI (1), Direct Input (1), Direct Injection (1)	1

Question No.	Answer	Mark
2(e)	It will pick up less of the finger and fret noise than a microphone (1), it will offer a different tone to a microphone (1) and will not pick up the room that the instrument is played in (1)	1

Question No.	Answer	Mark
2(f)	Bar 11 – a strum or strumming (1) Bar 15 – slide up in pitch (1) or slide down the fret board towards the sound hole (1), also allow 'string bend'	2

Question No.	Answer	Mark
2(g)	It will sound up a tone (two semitones) (1). It will sound up in pitch at the full bend range of the instrument's default settings (1) It will sound up in pitch (1)	1

Question No.	Answer	Mark
2(h)	45	1

Question 3 (9 marks)

Question No.	Answer	Mark
3(a)	Listen to candidate file 'TK3 Merc EXAMPLE mix.wav'	
	Excellent – all creaking floors and knock sounds are removed, from bar 24 to the end	4
	Good – the bass line is intact with no new problems, but some noise is still present	3
	Poor – noise has been removed but so has a very small section from the end of the bass line	2
	Extremely poor – noise is still present and or much of the bass line has been disturbed	1
	File is not part of mix track or no mix track exists	0

Question No.	Answer	Mark
3(b)	A cross-fade lowers the volume of the first track (1) while at the same time raising the volume of the second track (1) to create a single seamless take/ track (1) or Candidate could reference: in analogue tape, a cross-fade is an angled cut in once piece of tape, take 1 (1), followed by an exact opposite angled cut in a second piece of tape, take 2 (1) the two pieces of tape are spliced or joined to create a single seamless take (1)	3

Question No.	Answer	Mark
3(c)	Multi-velocity sampling is the process for recording the same note/pitch (A=440 Hz for example) or hit on the same instrument (1) at many different dynamic levels (pp, p, mp, mf, f, ff for example) (1). Each different strike captures unique and different aspects of the instrument's sound and acoustic response. (1) Harder-hit notes are often brighter (1)	2

Question 4 (16 marks)

The answers given below are intended as a guide. Alternative answers will always receive credit if they form an accurate and unambiguous response to the question posed. The mark total awarded for this question is 16. Please note, more than 16 possible marks are listed here.

An analogue to digital, A/D converter is used to turn changes in an electrical/analogue signal/voltage into a digital signal (1) – a stream of 0s and 1s / binary data (1). As digital it can be stored to digital media such as a hard disc or CD (1). A digital-to-analogue converter (D/A converter) is used to turn the data back into analogue for playback via speakers (1).

The process by which most A/D converters work is called **PCM** (1) or pulse code modulation (1).

Sample rate (1) is the number of times a second a measurement of amplitude is captured (1). Bit depth (1) is the precision of each of those measurements of amplitude (1). Sample rate is often expressed in Hertz, Hz, kiloHertz, kHz or cycles per second (1). Common sample rates include: 44.1 kHz (CD quality) (1), 48 kHz (1), 96 kHz (1) and 192 kHz (1). Higher sample rates allow a more faithful representation of the original wave to be captured (1) but use more memory/RAM (1).

Nyquist theorem (1) states that the sample rate of an A/D should be at least twice the rate of the highest audio frequency or harmonic to be recorded in order to achieve a good quality recording (2). When the sample rate is not high enough **aliasing** occurs (1). Aliasing introduces audible noise at a lower frequency then the incoming analogue audio, even if the incoming audio is above the audible frequency range (1).

To prevent aliasing noise, most analogue-to-digital filters incorporate an **anti-aliasing filter** (1). This comprises a low pass filter (1) before the A/D converter (1) to remove any harmonics or frequencies of the incoming wave that are over half the frequency of the sample rate (1). For example in an audio CD recorder a low pass filter of 20 kHz is placed before the A/D converter (1), as the maximum sample rate for a standard audio CD is 44.1 kHz. The sample rate of 44.1 kHz was chosen for digital audio CDs as it is just over twice the highest audio frequency humans can hear, approximately 20 kHz (1), and satisfies the Nyquist theory as a result.

Bit depth determines the peak dynamic range of the input signal (1). Standard bit depths are: 8-bit (1) (low resolution), 16-bit (1) (CD-quality resolution), 24-bit (1) (recording studio resolution). Any sample of the wave that does not fit exactly onto one of these levels (bits) or steps must be rounded up or down (1). This process is called **quantisation** (1): the result when played back is distortion of that part of the recording, as the original natural shape of the wave is altered (1). The higher the bit depth, the smaller the quantisation error and better the quality of sound (1).

Another way to alleviate quantisation distortion in an A/D converter is a process called **audio dithering** (1). Audio dithering introduces a small amount of noise, low-level hiss, to reduce distortion (1). The pay off is a slight reduction in signal-to-noise ratio (1).

Once set, in theory an A/D converter's sample rate does not vary. However, in practice sample rate variation does occur; this is called **jitter** (1). Jitter is caused by variation in the oscillator that sets the clock or sample rate (1). Modern A/D converters incorporate high quality internal PLL (1) (phase lock loop) chips to help eliminate jitter (1).

Question 5 (18 marks)

Listen to file 'TK3 Merc EXAMPLE mix.wav' before marking answers.

Please note: when marking this paper, do not double-assess the noisy bass ending. If the noise has not been cut out the candidate should only lose marks in question 3a, not in this question as well.

(5a) (3 marks)

Marks	Management and controlling EQ of drum
3	Excellent control so that the drums sit in the mix without extreme frequency exaggeration or restriction. (NOTE: A high frequency boost EQ from approximately 500 Hz up should have been added to compensate for the dull drums – listen to the cymbals for this)
2	Competently handled with some misjudgements, drums occasionally lack for presence or boom
1	EQ applied poorly, with extreme settings. Lows, mids or highs boom or are too shrill, or are over-emphasised
0	No EQ can be identified, or as the original file No mix present on CD

(5b) (3 marks)

Marks	Management and controlling dynamics, vocal
3	Excellent control so that the vocal sits in the mix and the detail in the quieter sections is brought out; no pumping or squashed sound. The vocal is even and smooth
2	Competently handled but the vocal occasionally sounds squashed, pumps or jumps out too much
1	Poorly handled so that vocal sounds squashed, pumps or jump out, and does not sit well in the mix
0	No compression can be identified on the vocal No mix present on CD

(5c) (3 marks)

Marks	Management and control of stereo delay on the guitar
3	Excellent use of stereo delay effect enhances interest in the mix at the start of the guitar
2	Competent stereo delay, but is too extreme or subtle
1	Poorly managed delay that has too much feedback, or is too fast, or is barely noticeable
0	No stereo pan can be heard on the guitar or it is added elsewhere in the track No mix present on CD

(5d) (3 marks)

Marks	Application of reverb
3	Excellent use of reverb on all tracks. (NOTE: It is unlikely that a reverb time of more than 1.2 seconds would be appropriate for this track.)
2	Competent use of reverb with some misjudgements
1	Serious misjudgement on one or more tracks. Vocal is swamped or reverb has been added to the bass in significant amounts to wash out the track or make it sound too distant for example
0	No use of reverb on any track No mix present on CD

(5e) (3 marks)

Marks	Balance and blend
3	Consistently well balanced and effectively blended across all parts of the mix. (NOTE: Each track should be clearly heard. However, the vocal should be slightly forward in the mix)
2	Most tracks are well balanced. A minor slip in one part
1	Poorly balanced, detrimental to the musical outcome. Vocal back in mix or one instrument too loud
0	Not all tracks present No mix on CD

(5f) (3 marks)

Marks	Presentation of mix
3	Beginning and end of mix does not cut out music, the reverb tail or end of cymbals. The beginning should have 0.2–1 seconds of silence before the music starts. The mix output should be near normalised with no distortion
2	Beginning and end of mix does not cut out music or reverb tail or cymbals. The beginning has a silence of greater than 1 second. The mix output should be near normalised with no distortion
1	Beginning and end of mix does not cut out music. Reverb tail or a small section of the cymbals may be slightly cut off. The beginning has a silence of greater than 1 second. The mix output is too low or too high or in places distorts
0	Parts of the song are missing, e.g. cut off at the start/end. The mix output is too low or too high or consistently distorts No mix present on CD